Love and Deception

One Family's Encounter with Dementia

A NOVEL

J. Steven Hunt

PUBLISHED BY

CREATIVE PRODUCTS
AND SERVICES

ISBN **978-1503171800**

Published by JSH Creative Products and Services

Printed by Createspace

First Edition

Dedication

To my wife, Kathy, who gave me wisdom, love and patience
during the difficult years of her mother-in-law's
dementia, and during my long hours
writing of this story.

Acknowledgments

I am indebted to my friend and publishing advisor,
David Sanford, for his gracious help.

Hats off to my friend and fellow author,
Nancy Hedberg, and to Corban University
journalism professor, Dr. Marty Trammell,
for their steadfast encouragement.

Grateful thanks to colleagues Rebekah Benham for
her outstanding editing help, and Ellen Kersey for
her guidance through the perils of punctuation.

Special thanks to Judy Belt and Kim Sessa from
Lancaster Village Assisted Living Center in Salem,
Oregon, and Marie Chin and the staff at Marian
Estates Nursing Home in Sublimity, Oregon for the
loving care they gave to my mother during the
15 years of dementia and the difficult,
closing months of her final journey.

J. Steven Hunt

Preface

This book, although a work of fiction, is loosely based on the true story of the author's family history and experience with eldercare and dementia. The Alzheimer's Association describes dementia as "a general term for a decline in mental ability severe enough to interfere with daily life."

Memory loss is an example. It is caused by physical changes in the brain. Alzheimer's disease is the most common type of dementia, accounting for 60 to 80 percent of cases. The top ten signs and symptoms are listed as:

Memory loss
Difficulty performing familiar tasks
Problems with language
Disorientation to time and place
Poor or decreased judgment
Problems with abstract thinking
Misplaced things
Change in mood or behavior
Changes in personality
Loss of initiative

For further information on dementia go to: alz.org

———

A PORTION OF THE AUTHOR'S INCOME FROM THIS BOOK IS BEING DONATED TO THE ALZHEIMER'S ASSOCIATION.

Introduction

For four generations, Mom's family history played out on their Colorado ranch. The family endured many circumstances to survive, but her most difficult challenge was from an intangible force. It came into her home late in life as an uninvited guest. It was dementia and it came to redefine my mother's life and impact mine as well. Back then it seemed to hit us unfairly, like a sucker punch, but in time I came to accept it as just a reality of life.

This is the story of our journey—Mom and me mostly, but other family members as well. It is also the story of thousands of families whose experiences mirror ours. Dementia's grip turns two worlds upside down—the patient and the caregiver, and it drastically changes family dynamics. It disrupts the established pattern of leadership within longtime marriages or inverts parent/child roles.

Families whose loved one draws the dementia card are usually unprepared for it. They often build up resentment for distasteful encounters and blame themselves or other family members for bad things that occur. Tug-of-wars between siblings who must decide which one will help Mom or Dad can destroy relationships. Sometimes the symptoms are ignored and the patient suffers unnecessarily.

When we identified the disease, my approach was to move with it instead of pretending it didn't exist. But I often did things that seemed contradictory to my value system—something I named "loving deception." I had to departmentalize my thinking so I could understand who I was dealing with—Mom or the disease. I resigned myself to use deceit as a valuable tool to combat the illogical actions caused by dementia.

After my own experience, and hearing similar stories from my friends and acquaintances, I was amazed to realize how many of us were struggling with the same textbook issues of eldercare. I hope my story will encourage those who are among the ranks of volunteer caregivers. May it guard you against the feelings of frustration, sadness, guilt and resentment that can impact even a strong family. I hope you can instead experience a sense of purpose and accomplishment.

As you begin your role as caregiver, please don't walk out after the first act. Stay to complete the drama and serve your loved one and extended family well.

Prologue
1997

I am rushing through traffic thinking about deadlines. In the advertising business, time is money and I am using precious time to take Mom out to lunch. For the last several years I've taken care of her, but I don't feel I do a fair job of it. I visit her, and before I know it, she's spent another three weeks alone in the gloom of winter days.

My dad is gone, so apart from me she has no other family members nearby. I reserve Tuesdays to get her out of the care home and enjoy good ol' junk food with me. My work appointments aren't usually heavy that day and the routine makes it easy to remember I am going out for Tuesdays with Mama.

I now own The Mark Sanders Design Group. I started in the creative business as a teenager, doing mailbox lettering that led to weekly window banner painting and more. By the time I graduated, I was working four jobs—farm work, banner painting, highway signs and freelance art work. I soon discovered I liked doing art more than farming and hung out a sign at the entrance of our farm to advertise my willingness to trade art for money.

In college I worked at a gas station the first year and then, after my sports fan banners caught the eye of a printing director, I worked as a graphic designer. Work always seemed to find me—and soon I was into my career track without even realizing it. That was true of my dating life too. After meeting a petite, blue-eyed girl my freshman year, I married her two years later. Jamie is creative in her own right and an important part of the design group.

Life now moves at an incredibly hectic pace. Doing Tuesday lunch does not feel like an obligation any more. It's a welcome relief that helps me slow down and smell the roses—or in this case, the old folks' home.

Just ahead I see the tall cedar trees that mark the entrance to The MRC—what I call the beautiful Millwood Retirement Center. On the right side of the central parking lot is a long, two-story building for independent living. On the left is a large assisted living building nestled among the tall trees with its glass-covered turret gracing the dining area.

As I pull around the loading circle, I spot her there by the front door, sitting on an outside bench with a placid smile on her face. She's wearing her customary simple cotton dress, white sweater and not-so-color-coordinated black shoes. In her younger years her hair was long—waist-length to be exact—but now it's short for ease of care.

Even though I come every week, Mom doesn't know my car. Her dementia has dulled her recognition of many things. I always bounce out and yell, "Hi, Mom!" so she'll recognize me. Tuesday also happens to be the day for her hair appointment at the MRC salon. We coordinate things so that, a) she is routed out of hibernation for the appointment and b) the hairdresser can encourage her with news of my imminent visit.

"Laura, you're going to lunch with your son today!"

This comes as a brand new concept for Mom each week and she responds with, "My son? You mean Mark? Oh my!"

"Yes, he'll be here in a few minutes, so you have to sit real still and let me do your hair," Alexis-the-hair-gal says.

Some days I arrive early and peek through the door. Alexis is carefully doing all she can to cut a few snips of hair during the wash and set treatment. Mom reacts strongly about getting any hair cut off, and if it happens, she remembers the indignity for some time after. Streetwise trickery is needed to apply the snipping because it's the only way her hair ever gets cut.

They are quite a pair—Mom in a nice dress and array of jewelry topped with big, lemon-yellow curlers and Alexis, the urban wild child, with her ensemble of obligatory tattoos and piercings. Why she chose to work with the geriatric crowd at a seniors' home is beyond me. But to her credit, she is better than her predecessors at handling Mom's idiosyncrasies.

Advancing dementia now controls a good part of Mom's life. It's hard to pin down when it started exactly, because early symptoms were difficult to recognize. For a while I was never quite sure if her memory loss was from old age or if her weird habits were just weird habits.

When she first came to Millwood, she had her quirks, but, like everyone else, we just chalked them up to lagging social skills. She became a part of the group dining experience, which was a sharp contrast to the time before group living when she ate alone. There are times when I eat lunch with her here—pretty nice, actually. But Mom isn't cut out for this crowd, most of whom moved here for the luxury retirement experience. Mom has always been just a plain and simple country girl and isn't interested in all the fuss.

She likes to go to the small library to sit quietly, reading the books she brings along. The library also serves as a chapel on Sundays, so it has become her favorite hangout. For a while she enjoyed going on weekly outings in the Millwood van, summer trips to the park, the Coast and various other tourist destinations. But after a while she just stopped going, and I wondered why. I assumed she'd reached a "been there, done that" stage and just dropped out.

As time passes, I realize her withdrawal is caused by the advancement of her dementia, and she feels frustrated with her loss of cognitive skills. With all of the commotion around her on the bus, she gets confused when a question is thrown at her, and then, in a defensive way, she pushes back with undue force that doesn't win friends and influence people. I feel helpless to advise her and have to accept the fact that I can't change her at this age.

So I find myself submerged in eldercare. I don't think of myself as an expert at it, but I've always had an overriding sense of obligation to take care of my folks. Since my siblings are scattered across the Western Hemisphere, I find myself walking solo through Dementiaville. In recent years Mom has adjusted to the assisted living routine, probably because the living style is matched to her current mental state.

She enjoys the group activities and dining hall experiences, but that's because she sits off to the side and watches other people do the activities. In the dining hall she shares a table with someone in a bib and asks to eat their Jell-o. Then she steals their silverware before returning to her room. Fortunately, up to now I've not seen any college-style food fights.

We are well into our sixth year at Millwood, and I've gotten our weekly outings down to a science. Each week I open her car door and she murmurs "thank you" like I am a charming suitor. After climbing in, she swipes her hand over her right shoulder several times before grasping the seatbelt. Then I start rolling and ask, "Do you want to get some lunch?"

She smiles and looks all sheepish and flattered that I am being so considerate to take her out. "How come we're doing this?" she asks.

"We do this every Tuesday, you know."

"We do?"

"Yup."

After a couple of blocks we turn onto the main boulevard. She gazes around and takes in the new surroundings like she's just stepped onto Mars.

"Just look at all those cars! Where are they all going?"

"Oh, uh…places to go, people to see I guess. They're just like us—going somewhere."

We drive a few more blocks, making our way through heavy traffic.

"Look at those cars! The wheels aren't even going around!"

"Well, actually they are, you just can't see the hubcaps spinning because they're all smooth."

"That's because they're not wagon spokes," I'm thinking.

Her amazed reply is simply, "Huh!"

We drive a few more blocks. Invariably there are people riding bikes on the sidewalk. She focuses on one and says, "There's that same man on the bike! We see him every time we come here!"

I respond in kind: "Huh!"

The recycling pattern of her mind fascinates me. No matter how many new things happen in front of her each week, she processes the same conversational patterns. She is upbeat and joyful about it and looking like she has the best life anyone could hope for.

Initially, I made the Tuesday menu choices, which were the same thing every week: two Junior Whoppers, two small fries and two senior drinks. I'm a fairly easy guy to please when it comes to food and Mom is just happy to spend time with me. When guilt about better nutrition got to me, I moved our venue to a new place down the street and amended the fare to turkey and veggie sandwiches with no fries.

Holidays are always complicated but we make every attempt to make them meaningful. The Fourth of July is one holiday that the Millwood staff does up right. It is a good old-fashioned, red-white-and-blue celebration featuring a guest musician—usually a guitarist who sings country or old-timey music. There's a big tent, red polka-dot hats and skirts, matching picnic tablecloths and lots of barbequed chicken. Even though our kids are doing fun things at the lake involving fireworks, Jamie and I commit to spend lunchtime with Mom, just to make her proud. But I have to be honest. When Mom says, "I'd better get back to my room," I don't argue too much because I'm human, and I welcome the opportunity to get back to my own family to finish the day with younger people who are doing far more exciting things.

Besides the weekly visits, my wife Jamie and I make sure Mom spends the major holidays with us. We live about ten miles west of Millwood over a complicated route, long bridge and multiple off-ramps, so we don't risk having her drive. While Jamie prepares dinner, I pick up Mom and enjoy a leisurely drive through town. That is half the fun for her.

"Where are we going?"

"My house," I say with a tinge of excitement in my voice.

"Oh good! What are we going to do?

"Did you know it's Thanksgiving?"

"Really?"

"Yes! So we're going to my house to have Thanksgiving dinner and see your grandkids!" She becomes engrossed in the scenery and forgets all that I've said. It's just a matter of time before we do it all over again.

"Where are we going?"

"My house!" I say it with a tinge of excitement in my voice.

"Oh good! What are we going to do?"

"Did you know it's Thanksgiving?............"

This usually goes on for as long as we drive. Sometimes I keep my answers identical just to see if she remembers the previous conversation. She rarely does.

By the time we arrive at the house, the kids and grandkids

are there, and she is met with multiple greetings and hugs. She just looks around with a big smile and drinks it all in. After finding her a seat in the corner I spend a little time in conversation.

"Whose place is this?"

"It's my house, Mom."

"Really? Oh, I should know that!"

Someone walks by and she looks at them and says, "Who's this?"

"I'm Katie!" my daughter says. "I'm your granddaughter."

"My granddaughter…? Oh my goodness! …What are we going to do?"

"It's Thanksgiving" someone says. "We're having dinner!"

We think of the outing as her great escape from boredom, but, as soon as the meal starts she begins suggesting that she needs to get back to Millwood before the doors are locked.

"It's okay Mom. We can just ring the bell and they'll let us in," I reassure her. But three or four minutes later she repeats her concerns. By the time the meal is finished (and she's had pie) her level of consternation has reached the point where it's just wiser to do as she asks. So, we grab our coats, say our goodbyes, and an hour after arriving, we're back on the 40-minute round trip to Millwood.

When people not-so-subtly suggest that Mom must be lonely, spending the holiday alone, it takes me awhile to get past the guilt they've heaped upon me. But I've talked to professionals who say that dementia patients are often most comfortable and fulfilled in their familiar surroundings.

8

Being a volunteer caregiver is a perpetual mix of emotions—love, frustration, obligation and ultimately fulfillment. But it is draining, and it took me a few years to come to terms with the emotional cycles. I use my sense of humor to get me through it all. When I go into smart-aleck mode, don't think of me as disrespectful or cynical about the plight of the elderly. I show a lot of restraint and respect in a multitude of difficult situations and reserve my humor for the times when I can step back and process things.

I remember once when the family all had a good laugh around an evening meal. I related an experience to them about how I was learning to be a proper assistant, balancing too much or not enough attention as Mom insisted on doing things herself.

We'd gone to a restaurant and settled into our meal when she said she needed to find a restroom. Remembering her propensity to get lost, I offered to go with her.

She looked flabbergasted and snapped, "Well, I can do it! Good night, I've been around a lot longer than you!"

"Okay," I smiled (on the outside).

She did find the restroom on her own, partly because of the big sign on the wall that said RESTROOMS. But coming back was a different story. For a person who often sees "that same man on the bike," I've noted that faces seem to be less familiar than restroom signs.

I watched from across the way as she came out of a doorway kind of absent-mindedly and suddenly stopped as her internal navigation system went on "you're lost" alert. She tried to cover her feeling of uncertainty and smiled at a nearby couple as she hurried forward. Then she stopped as her navigation system again went on red alert. She repeated the same scenario every few feet. My inclination to help was strong, but I was reminded of her "been around longer than you" statement, so I refrained from diving in.

Finally, a server noticed her dilemma and asked if help was needed. After an exchange of words, Mom's new helper looked around the room. I waved my hand with a friendly little smile and caught their attention.

As Mom slid back into our booth, I asked how it went. From her answer I gathered that upon leaving the restroom she had stumbled into a hallway that led to a kitchen storage room. She said she found some of her favorite pie there and had a little taste (or two) before making her way out.

That's the way life has gone for a few years now. As I look back on the big picture I wonder how we've made it. Our family has always been stable and strong. But life has thrown a lot in our pathway at times. They say Alzheimer's is "the long goodbye" and we begin to view our journey based on the last few, difficult years. It's easy to forget the many beautiful things that led up to this difficult season of life.

In Mom's case there were *many* wonderful things that shaped her life. I was about six when she began sharing the oral history of our family. For me, her stories were better than books about pirates and cowboys, and the best part was her stories were true. She'd say, "Mark! It's time for bed!"

After implementing the usual delay tactics, I'd resign myself to climb into bed and scrunch under the covers while she tucked me in with a kiss. I loved the smell of her hair and her gentle mother's touch. Then I'd say my prayers. I had my own customized version of the familiar kids' prayer that went something like this: "Now I lay me down to sleep, I pray the Lord my soul to keep, God bless Momma-Daddy-Mark-Dave-Lisa-in-Jeez-name-amen!"

Sometimes I felt a bit guilty zipping through a prayer in rapid-fire fashion, but I told myself it was the thought that counted, and besides, I was now ready for story time.

Mom's narrative went back to the time of her grandparents, Nels and Marta Jensen, and her parents, Henry and Louise Jensen. She would look far off and sigh, as if shaking off the cares of the day, and begin to tell me each chapter of her family history…

Part One

LAURA RELATES THE STORY
OF HER EARLY FAMILY'S LIFE

1

BEGINNINGS

The four-mast *RMS Oceanic* sighted land in June 1871. It had begun in Portsmouth, England weeks earlier and labored toward New York with 1,000 passengers and 140 crew members on board. As the White Star Line's newest ship, it had created a lot of excitement when it left port. My grandparents, twenty-year-olds Nels Jensen and his bride Marta were on board. They had married in Norway a few weeks earlier and made their way to England to sail on to America, ready for whatever adventure lay ahead.

Marta had grown up in relative ease in a small Norwegian town that was home to her father's successful fishing business. It was at a summer outing along the Skarpesvingen waterway when she first saw Nels. He looked at her as she passed him along the rocks near the water's edge.

Marta was immediately attracted to his rugged build and strong face, and she wished for a way to meet him. From time to time that day, she found herself checking her hair and smoothing her skirt as he passed nearby. She tried to think of ways to increase her chances of meeting him.

But Nels took care of that. It wasn't long before he introduced himself and they began to spend more time together. As the outing concluded, they exchanged addresses, and, in spite of their newfound friendship, their goodbye was awkward. Each had felt strong attraction to the other and they promised to stay in touch.

In the months ahead, their letters made those communications easier, and in one, Nels shared his dream of going to America. He asked Marta to marry him and plan a life together there. Marta was torn between her love for Nels and her obligation to her father.

By now, her mother was gone, and her father was often away on fishing junkets. Their relationship was strained, and his moody anger issues often hurt her in a way that affected any chance of a close bond. But still she wanted to do right by him.

Nels had long since made his dream known to his parents, and for his part, he merely told them he was ready to make his way to America which they accepted without disagreement. There was an unspoken understanding that Nels was his own man, and in their minds, they had already assumed it was inevitable.

Marta knew finding a time to have a conversation with her father about marrying Nels would be difficult, even without the subject of leaving Norway. As she and Nels plotted their next move, it became apparent to them that waiting would accomplish nothing.

They agreed that Nels would pick Marta up at the clock tower near her home at midnight on March 3. They would then make their way south to the port city of Mandal and find a clergyman who would marry them. After that, they planned to board a boat to Denmark and make their way

16

south where they could cross the Channel to England.

When the appointed day arrived, Marta decided to abandon the idea of a conversation about leaving. She had carefully packed a small bag of belongings and nervously prepared dinner for her father. Her emotions were strong as she wrestled with feelings of guilt about leaving him, and the strong love in her heart that drew her to Nels. She was not accustomed to either emotion and her stomach was tied in knots as she waited for the evening to pass.

Before bed, she kissed her father goodnight and told him she loved him. He seemed surprised at her hug that lasted longer than usual. Upstairs, Marta checked her bag and then lay on the bed, anxiously looking at her clock. She placed the note beside her bed that she'd written to her father, and then allowed herself to think about Nels.

An hour later, she confirmed the time as 11:00 p.m., and carefully crept down the stairs to ease herself through the weathered, ancient front door. Outside, the crisp air cut into her lungs as she made her way quickly away from the house.

She set out toward the tall clock tower visible in the distance. As she drew closer, she prayed no one would see her.

Suddenly, her heart jumped as a nearby dog's angry bark startled her. She quickly moved on and tried as best she could to stay out of sight, close to the walls of the street's darkened shops.

Leaving the protection of the shadows, she descended stairs that led to the base of the clock tower. From the darkened side of its massive stone foundation she saw a figure step forward and move toward her. Suddenly she was in Nels' arms, holding him in a joyful embrace. Nels kissed her, and following a brief, cherished interlude, he reluctantly turned his attention to beginning their arduous walk south.

The plan was to stay on the main roads and sleep in sheltering forests. After moving swiftly into the countryside, Nels slowed his gait and patiently paced himself to Marta's walking speed. But at times, he grew impatient and goaded her to forge ahead as her fatigue set in.

Their journey lasted three days and nights before they reached the port city of Mandal where they treated themselves to a hot meal at an eating house. After the short but welcome rest, they inquired about a local clergyman who might help them.

As good fortune would have it, there was a church only a short distance away. A friendly gentleman answered their knock and Marta immediately knew she liked him.

"Good afternoon," he said. "My name is Oscar. What brings you here today?"

"We are traveling and would like to ask if you would be kind enough to officiate our wedding ceremony," said Nels.

"Oh! It's a wedding we want is it? I think this is a perfect day for that!"

Oscar's warm greeting and bright smile shone as soon as they made their request, and he invited them to sit for coffee.

"So, what are your traveling plans?"

"We come from Lindesnes and we hope to soon sail to America," Nels replied with a slightly apologetic smile.

"Oh my goodness, those are mighty big plans!" Oscar said, without disguising his amazement.

18

"We have made this far just by walking each day for a week," Marta said as she shifted in her seat. "But we're looking forward to our new life in America once we're married."

Oscar shared with them his work as a clergyman which had covered most of his life.

"You sound like you're an adventurous couple," he said. "Follow me and you can tell me more."

After getting his Bible and ceremony book, Oscar showed them to a small chapel where they would have the ceremony. It was brief, but full of joy and hope and represented the first step in their dream of life together in America.

When it was finished, Nels kissed Marta.

"Congratulations Mrs. Jensen," he said as he smiled, momentarily forgetting Oscar.

Marta gazed into his eyes as her smile grew to a giggle.

"I'm thankful you stopped here today," Oscar said. "It was going to be a quiet day but you've made it a memorable one."

Oscar graciously refused to accept a fee, and went even further to make them feel welcomed. He invited them to use a small guest house behind the church for their honeymoon that night.

It was so wonderful to have found such a perfect place for their wedding, and the guest house was such a welcome surprise. Marta wished for more time to rest from their journey, but she knew they must press on. Nels was determined to find a boat headed to Denmark.

The next day Oscar sent them away with bread and cheese and best wishes for their travels.

After a month of travel, their dream of setting sail for America was close at hand. As they arrived in Portsmouth, *Oceanic* loomed large above them at the wharf. They steadily worked their way into the line of people, moving forward through the process of buying passage and boarding the ship, edging closer to what would be their most important journey ever.

Once on board, the sights, sounds and smells of this adventure were sometimes overwhelming. Marta looked all around her as she tried to take them all in. As the mooring ropes were released, they held their gaze on what would be their last view of England.

"Will we have our own bed?" Marta wanted to know.

Neither had sailed before, but Nels knew better than to expect too much.

"We will be fine, Marta," he promised. His reply held a tone of finality, revealing his hope of ending her myriad of questions. But he avoided meeting her eyes in case his face betrayed his inner uncertainties.

Arriving below deck, they found that standing up in their living space was impossible for Nels, who was a strapping six-foot-three-inches tall. But he had learned to meet challenges of any kind without wavering and took the condition of their quarters in stride.

Nels' appearance was deceiving. His face was thin and angular but he had a ruggedness and strength about him from years of farm work. For protection from the salty wind, he wore heavy canvas pants and a bulky coat, making him appear even larger. He went about things with a quiet confidence, and although he didn't show it, he was excited to be on his way to fulfill his dreams. His thoughts turned now to Marta and the responsibility he had to keep her safe.

Marta was a small, slightly-built girl, and he realized each day how dependent on him she would be. Her blonde hair was usually pinned to the top of her head, giving her a mature appearance. Her ready smile and kind nature revealed her gentle spirit.

As the ship made its way out to open water, they did what was possible to make their cramped living quarters livable in the increasingly rough seas. On this, her first seafaring trip, Marta's stomach reacted violently to the rolling motion of the waves. She spent much of her time running to the deck railing to offer the contents of her stomach to the fish.

Everything was an adjustment at sea. Some, who were adversely affected by nausea, spent the entire journey in bed. Marta watched in horror as, day after day, some passengers with overwhelming seasickness starved to death due to the inability to hold nourishment down.

There was no refrigeration for food on board, so passengers lived on salted pork, dried fish, ships biscuit and hard cheese. The food was strictly rationed by the galley staff. It was either eaten standing up or sitting wherever passengers could find an open spot.

Below deck, Nels used a travel trunk as a table. In doing so, they carved out what was essentially a small dining area. Marta preferred to stay near the safety of solid walls and posts so that she had something to steady herself. With only three quarts of water per week for each of them, she adapted to the regimen and gradually got her sea legs. She learned to stabilize her stomach by adhering to a diet of dried meat and wine.

Nels did his best to look out for Marta, covering the day-to-day errands for her, and finding ways to keep her comfortable in their small quarters. As the days passed, Marta was at last able to venture out and explore their surroundings.

She met other women on board and found a best friend—a young Norwegian named Elsa, who was just eighteen and traveling with a guardian. Elsa's parents had sent for her after they had left months earlier to establish a home in America.

The guardian was a woman named Gerta, who operated with a military precision well-suited for the job. But Elsa felt smothered by Gerta's constant surveillance and looked for fun and exciting things to do. Befriending Marta was a welcome relief because she invented even more schemes for Elsa to escape Gerta's grasp.

One evening following dinner, Marta invited Elsa to her cabin for some girl talk. They waited at a distance before Gerta averted her gaze long enough for them to slip down a passageway. With no light except a candle, the girls spent the evening in the semi-darkness of the moonlit ocean, sharing their hopes and dreams. When Elsa finally returned to her quarters, she encountered an angry Gerta, but the benefits of her time with Marta outweighed the scolding she had to endure.

Week after week *Oceanic* sailed on, and the lack of privacy, cramped living quarters and illness took its toll. Passengers found ways to combat the drudgery, sometimes dancing on deck, writing letters or playing games. Despite the difficulties, they were kept going by the prospect of their arrival in

America.

Nels busied himself making notations about the work he would need to do after arriving at their destination. He planned the details for living in New York, finding wagon trains headed west and the ultimate dream of buying land. One morning he heard commotion on deck and after going there, was told that land was in sight.

With New York at hand, Marta and Nels began preparations for disembarking. Marta ran to find Elsa and, after searching the deck full of passengers, saw her with Gerta, intently looking at the horizon. As Marta approached, Elsa met her and they hugged with best wishes, tearfully promising to stay in touch. Soon they were engulfed in the chaotic rush of passengers getting off the ship.

2

AMERICA

Nels and Marta clung to each other as the gangplanks were dropped and passengers began pushing their way down to the dock. Along with excitement came a feeling of anxiety about their new adventure. Marta had hoped to keep Elsa in sight, but Gerta held her back, and Marta soon lost her in the sea of humanity.

They were jostled along the dock and then pushed faster down a narrow street, dodging other passengers as they surged ahead on welcome dry land. Marta struggled to keep pace and carry her bag, so Nels reached down and took it from her grasp, lifting it high onto his shoulder.

His long strides soon moved him away from Marta, but she kept her baggage in sight. When Marta stumbled and almost fell, Nels decided to take a moment of refuge on a staircase.

"Can you go on?" Nels asked as he pulled her close to him.

"Yes!" Marta said bravely. Nels waited a few minutes and then stepped higher on the stairs for a better view of their surroundings. Up ahead, he saw immigrants gathered around a table, each hoping to receive housing permits.

"I can see where we need to go, Marta!" he cried. Marta grasped his coat as they pushed ahead. They found a place in line at the immigrant table a few minutes later. They prayed all would go well with getting a permit. A half hour later, the attendant finished processing their papers and pointed down a street toward a place assigned to them.

After their cramped quarters on the ship, the long streets of the city seemed endless and a little frightening. Strange sights and smells surrounded them, and their pace slowed as they tried to absorb it all. Marta was uncomfortable as she sensed the gazes of shop owners assessing them as they walked. Her clothing and baggage gave her the telltale appearance of a newcomer, and she was again thankful for Nels' steadying presence.

After climbing to a second-level balcony, they found their small room. Nels opened the door to reveal a dusty wooden floor with two chairs and a table, a bed and a small sink below empty pantry shelves. A small fireplace in the corner would serve as a stove for both heating and cooking.

They were so tired from their journey that they sank onto the bed with a sigh and fell back, happy to have successfully made it to America.

"Well, Marta, what do you think of your crazy husband now?" Nels beamed. Marta rolled her eyes and soon they were laughing. Nels shook her in a playful bear hug and they fell from the bed, shrieking with laughter as they landed on the floor. Being truly alone for the first time in weeks felt exhilarating, and they became lost in each other's arms.

With the coming darkness, they turned to the task of unpacking their belongings. Nels checked to see if their nest egg was safe. It was there—almost a half year's salary he had saved for the trip.

Without the availability of banks, Nels had hidden his money in his underwear behind his belt buckle. He carefully took a few bills out whenever they needed money, and on this day they intended to use it for the fresh food they had gone without for so long.

In the fading light they locked their door and descended into a street filled with fruit and vegetable stands and an amazing amount of things to see. There were so many immigrant shop owners selling apples, bananas, carrots, beans and corn that Marta couldn't believe her eyes. After the steady diet of salty meat for several weeks, she couldn't wait to get back to their flat and enjoy fresh food.

As the Jensens stayed close to their stark surroundings in the following weeks, their routine became easier. But they never lost sight of their goal to move west as soon as they could. Each day in the marketplace they watched for a chance to connect with others who shared the same passion to travel westward.

One afternoon Marta was in search of produce for their meals. As she spotted what she wanted, another woman reached for the same bundle of vegetables.

"Oh!" they laughed nervously as each stepped back.

"Here! You should take them," said Marta as she saw her counterpart's embarrassment.

"Thank you…Oh!... my name is Sonja! I am from

Norway. And where are *you* from?" she inquired.

"We have come from Lindesnes and we are going to Minnesota!"

"Me too!" Sonja gasped. "When are you leaving?"

"Oh! We are waiting so long, so we are hoping to go as soon as we can. Wouldn't it be nice if we can travel together and become good friends?"

"Oh, yes! That would be wonderful!" Sonja cried. They hugged in excitement, and before the day was out, they had shared many stories about the things they found in common. Marta felt so good about having a friend. Sonja seemed to help the time pass more quickly as they counted the days till they would leave New York.

A few weeks later, the Jensens were among those in a wagon train heading out in a chain migration with other Norwegians.

Their route took them around the Great Lakes, following the railroad lines and sometimes the Mississippi River, past Illinois and Wisconsin. Heading through the wide grasslands of Minnesota, they discovered vista after vista of the new land. The soil was fertile and water was abundant, with lakes so prevalent it was hard to view the landscape without seeing one.

Gradually, the traveling group began to diminish as, one by one, families said farewell to their traveling companions and pulled away to head for their homestead claims. Sonja and her husband were among them, and Marta found herself again saying goodbye to another friend.

Nels bought a small piece of land at the claims office in

Minneapolis and a new horse they named Dag. They traveled northward for twelve more days as Nels checked his charts to calculate the location of their land. Marta was exhausted, but the joy of their dream kept her spirit buoyed.

Late one evening their destination came into view from the crest of a hill. It was such a beautiful sight! Nels jumped from the wagon and walked the land for the rest of the journey. It was hard to believe they had finally arrived at their farm in America.

The land contained an abandoned shack tucked into a coulee—a shallow swale of lower grassland that sloped down just enough to shelter them from cold winter winds. Prairie grass enveloped the shack, and as Nels approached, he cautiously pushed the door open, wary of any animal that may have taken up residence.

Stepping inside, the sweet smell of dirt and naturally-aged logs met them, and they were relieved to see it was in surprisingly good condition. It was solid, apart from many shafts of daylight poking through gaps in the walls.

For most of their first month, they spent their waking hours reworking the shack into a small, sturdy cabin. That summer Nels also planted corn and built fences for their animals, while Marta scrubbed and arranged the interior of the house into "something respectable."

They settled into a life mixed with both hardship and fulfillment. The unrelenting winters kept them hunkered down in their tiny cabin for weeks with nothing to do but wait it out. Nels gathered a lot of wood throughout the summers and stockpiled it behind their living quarters. Besides the obvious use for heat, it also served to insulate the back wall of the cabin from the blowing snow.

In the evenings they often warmed flat rocks on the fireplace hearth and used them as foot warmers in bed during the cold winter nights.

They adjusted to pioneer life with determination and purpose, and life was ever-changing with adventure never far away. Keeping a supply of fresh water required daily treks to the lake about a quarter mile away. Summertime treks were more enjoyable as Nels fell into a routine of leaving for the lake in early morning. He took advantage of the opportunity to hunt game along the way.

His routine was to first replenish the wood in the fireplace, then load his rifle and saddle the horse. He hung the leather water bags on his saddle, and after re-checking his gear, he encouraged Dag onto the trail.

As he headed out one morning in the third year on their Minnesota land, the spring thaw had begun and the trails were muddy. He arrived at a spot where a grove of trees opened to the lake, an especially beautiful place just after sunrise.

Moving carefully, he directed his gaze ahead, watching for game. Soon he sensed something in the air. Pulling up, he looked closer and saw a deer about a hundred yards away, drinking at the water's edge. He sat quietly and surveyed his options.

A slight movement to his right suddenly caught his attention just as he felt Dag tense. A bear was ambling toward the water, headed for the unsuspecting deer. Nels swore under his breath, disgusted with the intrusion, but was determined not to lose his chance to bag some meat. He quickly drew a bead and fired at the deer. It immediately hit the ground, but in spite of the rifle's explosion, the bear kept moving ahead.

The gunshot did, however, spook Dag, and in an instant, Nels found himself on the ground looking at the horse's rump as Dag galloped away.

Meanwhile, the bear, upwind from him, reared up but could neither smell nor see Nels. Glad for his luck, Nels laid low for a moment, waiting for things to quiet down. Mr. Bear soon smelled fresh meat and again turned toward his tempting venison breakfast.

There was no way on God's green earth that Nels was going to give up his rightful supply of fresh meat. In a burst of determination he stood up, took aim at the bear and pulled the trigger.

The report echoed and re-echoed through the timber, and as the smoke cleared, he saw the bear rear up on its hind legs. Call it bad angle, bad shot or just bad luck—the bullet missed its kill mark. As the bear swung around, it saw Nels and hurled headlong toward him in a charge intended to take out the threat.

At that point, Nels was caught off guard and turned to find safety. But fear and an overdose of adrenalin caused him to simply spin his wheels as he slipped in the muddy grass. He fell, dropping the rifle, and landed in a heap near a large tree.

In all the commotion, his pants had slipped to his knees and bound up his legs. He was now in a fix, and as the bear closed in, Nels did a desperate "caterpillar skooch" to reach his rifle and prepare to shoot.

BOOM! The rifle's report exploded and again the echo crashed its way through the timbered surroundings. This time the fast-moving bear howled with anger. The momentum of the charge propelled its now lifeless carcass forward and onto Nels as it dropped. He felt the pain of the crushing weight on his legs, and began working feverishly to pull free.

It took several minutes to move out from under the furry, 400-pound mass. He could smell foul bear breath as it escaped from the deflating lungs, submitting to death. At last, his legs slipped free and he was overwhelmed with relief. He was so excited about bagging both a bear and a deer that he didn't care about pain or bear breath.

"Yooooo hoo! I bagged two today!" he howled out loud. He limped around the carcass on his aching legs, thinking about his prize. After a minute his adrenaline rush crashed, and he sank back to the ground again. He laid on his back for several minutes to regain his strength.

After skinning both animals, he turned his attention to Dag. He spotted him at a distance, contentedly grazing on sweet grass. As he quietly moved toward him, Nels' mood was too good to be mad, even after being bucked off, and he simply greeted Dag with a reassuring stroke on his neck. He quartered the deer and bear, and loaded the meat onto his saddle, securing it with his rope.

Finally, he walked over to the lake to take care of his original purpose—getting water. As he filled his worn deerskin bags and tied their drawstrings, he felt happy about all that he'd accomplished. He headed for home where he would share his good fortune with Marta.

Marta's life on the homestead was rugged. Meals had to be prepared with only a fire and hearth to cook on. Without a way to keep meat fresh, Nels did the butchering outside and then dried the venison as jerky in the summer.

In winter months he packed the frozen quarters in a wooden box nailed high on the side of the house to keep it away from predators. It supplied them with meat for the winter months, and Marta cooked a variety of venison stews—Nels' favorite dish.

About 10 miles from the farm was a small town named Dale. There was a general store there, a saloon, a school and Fish Lake Lutheran Church. They went to town once a month, covering the long journey on horseback or in the wagon.

The trip required an early start, just after Nels' water trek and breakfast. In many respects it was invigorating to get out of the small shack and see friends in town. Marta bought cooking supplies and summer vegetables at the store. She often bought extra potatoes, butter and heavy cream to make Nels his lefse. Oh, how he loved his lefse!

When Nels made his water trips, Marta would get up early to make lefse. It was her way of showing her love and loyalty to Nels and she enjoyed seeing his wide smile and receiving his gentle swat on her backside as he thanked her for her thoughtfulness. Marta remembered, as a child, helping her mother make lefse.

She cooked the potatoes and ran them through a potato ricer. Then, she'd beat the butter, cream, salt and sugar to death and add them to the mashed potatoes and flour. Rolling out the dough into flat lefse pancakes was the last step before frying them on the griddle. It wasn't easy on an open fire, but Marta was now a master at it!

One morning in August, Nels was returning from his water trip, looking forward to the aroma of a warm, fresh batch of lefse. As he entered the cabin, he immediately sensed something was wrong. As his eyes adjusted to the darkened room, he saw Marta sitting on the bed soaking her foot in a pan of water.

"Marta?" he called out. Then he saw her reddened foot, painfully burned.

"Oh Nels," she sobbed, splashing water on her leg to ease her misery. "It hurts so badly!"

"What happened?" Nels asked as he sank to his knees, looking into her face.

"I was boiling water over the fireplace, and when I tried to move the kettle, it slipped and spilled scalding water on my leg."

"You sit back now," Nels said as he held her arm and attempted to adjust her leg in the water. "Let me get you some salve." Nels worked hard to take care of Marta as best he could and tried to convince himself that all would be well.

"You'll be better soon!" he said, hoping for the best. But, after two days, the burns looked worse, and he realized Marta would need a doctor's help. He carefully helped Marta wrap her foot and bundle up for the trip, then quickly harnessed the horse and hooked up the wagon to set out for Dale.

Moving across the rutted prairie was slow going and he saw Marta suffer as she lay in the wagon. He struggled to hold back desperate tears and feelings of despair, watching the love of his life in so much pain.

"Hold steady Marta!" Nels called as he looked back at her. Marta moaned a response and Nels could tell she was barely awake. By the time they arrived in Dale, she had slipped into unconsciousness.

After guiding the cumbersome wagon to the back street, they arrived at the doctor's house, a white clapboard building with a wide porch. A small, neat sign displayed the name Mark Wills, M.D.

Nels jumped from the wagon and headed for the porch. He knocked loudly, hoping to communicate urgency. A woman answered the door.

"May I help you?" she inquired.

"Yes, my wife is burned! I need the doctor!" Nels said, louder than he'd intended.

"The doctor is not in today," came the reply. "He was called out of town and won't be back for a few days."

"Can you help?" Nels asked, hopefully.

"Yes, she can come in and rest here, but I don't have anything I can do otherwise. I don't know anyone else in town who can help, either. My name is Lucy, by the way," she smiled.

"I am Nels and my wife is Marta." He was distracted with his concerns and was barely aware of what the woman said.

He returned to the wagon and carried Marta into the house. He laid her on a small cot and covered her with a light blanket. Nels knew the situation was serious, but there was simply no one to help. In desperation, he made his way to the general store to see if he could buy something—anything—

to apply as a salve remedy. The only treatments the store owner could recommend were those used for both animals and humans. So Nels agreed that it would be worth trying the veterinary salve in a desperate attempt to help.

"Marta, I'm going to put some salve on your leg," he whispered, receiving no response.

"What do you think, Mam?" he asked as Lucy seated herself beside Marta and busied herself by applying a cold cloth to Marta's forehead.

"It looks very serious, I must admit, and I'm sorry I can't offer more."

By late afternoon, Nels knew that he needed to get a head start on the long trip home. But he continued to apply the salve to Marta's leg and, after giving her something to eat, finally made the decision to head for home.

Over the next few days Marta drifted in and out of consciousness. She didn't understand her fate, and Nels reassured her that she would be fine. He could not bring himself to tell her the truth, but instead tried to conceal his concerns and encourage her in the midst of his looming dread.

As the night closed in she continued to lose ground as infection continued its rampage. A week later, when Nels returned from his early morning water trip, he found Marta lifeless on the bed.

For weeks Nels was so distraught he became hopelessly lost in sorrow. After Marta's death, he lost the will to work or eat and retreated into a dark world of depression and alcohol. For long periods of time he just sat outside the cabin and stared at the horizon.

The final chapter of their brief adventure in America came about three months after Marta's death. New immigrant travelers stopped by, looking for a place to settle.

As they looked through the shack and surrounding land that had once had been dear to Nels, he was unable to find any emotional connection to it, other than despair. He felt he had no reason to stay on at the place that only held heartbreak for him. He wasted no time in selling the farm and all of the things he and Marta had so carefully worked for since their arrival in America.

By late spring, Nels, at age 27, headed south with a bottle in his hand and no destination in mind.

3
HENRY

After Marta died in 1878, Nels lost his way for quite awhile. He developed a reputation as a rover and drifted through towns in Missouri and Oklahoma. He hired on for itinerant farm work and slept wherever he could, often in alleys or stables, drunk and dirty.

He eventually met a Cherokee woman named Inola at the local saloon in a town called Deer Creek. He was there to let off some steam and Inola immediately caught Nel's eye. She was a beauty among beasts, and soon they were drinking together. He didn't know if she was already spoken for, but he didn't ask questions. By the time they neared the end of the bottle, Inola's boyfriend, Jake, walked in and found them a little too cozy for his liking.

He was a big ol' boy with massive arms and a tattoo of a coiled rattlesnake on his hand. Folks called him "Jake the Snake," and as he made his way across the room, he pulled a knife. Nels, who was half drunk, unarmed and outsized, bravely fought back. But, in an instant, the knife sliced into his arm and he decided he'd had enough.

He high-tailed it out of there, making his way down the

street and forcing himself to keep moving in a desperate attempt to survive.

In the saloon, Jake turned his rage on Inola, filling the saloon with curses, and in a violent rage, pushed her to the floor before slamming his fist on the bar. He glared at the barkeep, demanding a drink.

Inola quickly moved out of the saloon, but she had seen something in Nels' fighting spirit that she liked. His strong but quiet manner was so healing compared to Jake's explosive anger.

Early the next day Inola found Nels holed up behind the livery, passed out from loss of blood. She set about to patch his arm, which now included a few new wounds. Once he was stabilized, Nels related to her that sometime during the night he'd encountered Jake on a darkened street and they had finished the fight. Nels got the upper hand, and while Jake was unconscious, Nels had helped himself to the rather large bankroll in The Snake's pockets. He figured the cash evened the score.

There was enough money in the stake to raise eyebrows and get him in trouble with the law, so Nels knew it was time to get out of town. But he felt a strong attraction to Inola and begged her to go with him. As strange as it seems, she agreed to go.

They quickly left Deer Creek and made their way to a canyon to hole up and decide what to do next. Nels knew this was his chance to make a clean start and Inola knew she wanted nothing more to do with Jake.

After three years of abuse and the dead end prospects at the Deer Creek saloon, she gained the courage to take a chance on Nels. So they continued westward and put distance between themselves and their troubles in Deer Creek.

Nels and Inola rode into to Rock Springs, Colorado in 1885, located a small country church and convinced the preacher to marry them. With the money Nels had "borrowed" from Jake and a surprising amount of money Inola had kept buried in her ample cleavage, they began to look for land. Even though Nels had wasted years as a drifter, he still had a hardened, wiry frame and didn't shy away from heavy farm work.

With renewed energy and a sense of purpose, the old Nels emerged and he threw himself into hard work, hoping to build a new life. He was soon a dependable ranch hand around Rock Springs and worked on several spreads, driving cattle, running threshing machines and caring for horses.

As he worked, he befriended an old rancher named Bernard Goertzen, who was looking to retire soon. Bernard took a real liking to Nels and Inola, and especially baby Henry, who was born around that time.

About two years later, old Bernard fell gravely ill. Inola stopped by every week to check on him and her attentive care made his pain bearable.

"Inola, I surely thank you for your kind help in caring for me," Bernard said weakly. I'm a lonely old man, and without you and Nels, I don't know where I'd be."

"I wouldn't have it any other way," she replied as she was leaving. "I'll see you next week unless I hear from you."

"Please bring Nels when you come back. I have something important I want to talk to you about," Bernard said with a wink and hint of a smile.

The following week, Nels and Inola stopped by for their visit. They found Bernard in bed as usual and each greeted him cheerfully.

"Good morning, Bernard! I hope your week has gone well. Anything you need? Sorry we haven't been back sooner."

"Oh, I've been as good as can be expected," Bernard said with a weak voice that was barely above a whisper. After attending to his medicine and beginning to fix some lunch, Inola returned to the room where Bernard lay.

"I have to talk about some things that I need to get off my chest," he said. "I need your help so you can take care of my place after I'm gone."

Bernard told Nels and Inola that he had no family and intended to will the ranch to them, lock, stock and barrel.

"I trust you two and I want the ranch to go forward in your hands. You can make it a real going concern again, and I'd be honored if you'd accept it."

Nels looked at Inola as he tried to comprehend the news.

"Are you sure, Bernard?" Isn't there anything we can do to make the terms a little more in your favor?"

"Nope. I have no use for it and I can't think of any better honor than to see you two thrive here.

Inola cared for him to the end, and after his death, they buried the old man on the ranch and used their money to carve out a new beginning on the place. They named it Jensen Ranch.

Nels threw himself into the development of the ranch as if to make up for lost time. The old man had let things fall apart when his health declined and Nels worked day and night to get it changed into a first-class operation.

The large ranch house needed a roof, better protection from winter snow and some sprucing up on the inside. Inola accepted the challenge for the inside and, like Marta's Minnesota cabin years before, made it homey and respectable.

Between high hills, the ranch spread across the valley in the shape of an undulating rectangle, randomly following the terrain. Never was there a more beautiful setting, with cattle scattered into the endless grazing fields that extended to the Rockies. Nels organized it into zones for grazing, hay crops and lanes for traffic routes to the back country. He repaired fences and barns and built new sheds and hutches for small animals.

Soon another boy, Austin, was born and the Jensens were well on their way to building the ranch into a dominant force around Rock Springs. Nels was proud of his boys, and as Henry grew older, he was given more than his share of the work. As the eldest, he was his father's protégé, but sometimes he felt the brunt of Nels' unrealistic demands, which only caused him to try extra hard to earn appreciation from his dad.

Austin was not his father's favorite. He was skinny and uncoordinated with an aversion to hard work. As the younger sibling he stayed close to his mother's side, and she defended his protests about doing farm work.

Henry didn't appreciate that he constantly had to finish Austin's jobs, and a resentment grew between the brothers. Whenever Henry attempted to make him finish his work, Austin weaseled out by claiming an injury or stomach ache.

Inola administered medical care for his concocted ills as he either stayed in bed or basked in the confines of the warm kitchen. Henry gave him the nickname "Austin the Possum."

By the time the Jensens had been on the ranch a few years, it hardly resembled the place they'd first inherited. The boys were growing, and Nels was a seasoned, respected rancher riding the crest of owning a beautiful, sprawling ranch.

One hot, summer day Henry was lazily walking along edge of the property when a visitor appeared in their long driveway. Henry's attention was drawn to him because the man was walking his horse in no apparent hurry.

As the rider drew closer, young Henry greeted him from the field with youthful enthusiasm. He asked if he could be of help. The man and horse appeared to have been traveling for awhile, showing the signs of road dust and fatigue.

"This is the Jensen Ranch, I'm told," the stranger said flatly. Henry assured him it was and proudly pointed out the far reaches of its perimeter.

"Who're you?"

"I'm Henry," he offered. He then prattled on, sharing more things than a stranger should be told. It never occurred to Henry to ask the stranger for his name or to state his business.

The stranger seemed unimpressed. He surveyed the landscape and focused on the ranch house and asked, "Yer folks home?"

"No, they went to town today—should be back later though." The stranger seemed to consider this and as he turned to leave, Henry noticed a tattoo of a snake on his hand. He watched as the horse and rider faded into the distance.

Later that evening when the family returned, Austin bailed out of the wagon before it stopped, and scurried off to play in the barn. As Henry greeted his parents, he tied the reins to the hitch and began unloading the wagon. He looked for help from Austin, but realized that idea was futile. His thoughts were on the stranger and the odd exchange he'd had with him. Nels asked about his day.

"We had a visitor this afternoon!" Henry explained.

"Yah? Asking directions?"

"No, he seemed pretty quiet and only asked who lived here. And then he just left."

"Wha'd he look like?"

"Oh…he was a big guy, kinda looked tired and dusty. Not really very friendly."

It wasn't until dinnertime that the subject returned. Inola started the conversation by again asking Henry how his day went. Henry explained that he'd spent a few hours working on fence repairs. He was proud that he had covered a lot of territory, his work ending near the road.

"I met a stranger today—kind of interesting guy," Henry said brightly. He went on to explain their exchange and that the man had a neat snake tattoo on his hand. He described how the snake's tail wound through his fingers. Inola said nothing, but inside, her heart stopped and she found it hard to breathe. She knew it had to be her old friend-turned-nemesis from the Oklahoma saloon days—the one they'd ditched in the livery.

As everyone retired for the night, Inola told Nels of her

suspicions. There was nothing they could do about it other than be wary in the event of trouble.

As fate would have it, it only took a couple of weeks for Trouble to come calling.

Early one morning Nels was feeding horses in the barn. He had routed Henry from his sleep, but so far had not seen him. Inola was up, preparing breakfast. It was a sunny, clear day, and she was expecting it to be hot as she opened windows to cool the house.

Austin was still asleep when Henry came downstairs, greeting Inola as he walked to the window. As he surveyed the yard, his eyes caught something out of place.

Past the wagon shed, along the back of the barn, he saw an unfamiliar horse, but his brain was still waking and his thoughts were dull. As he studied the horse, he realized that it looked like horse belonging to the stranger he'd met earlier.

"Hey, Mom! There's a horse out there. I think it belongs to that stranger I was telling you about."

Inola came to the window and looked out. Suddenly she grabbed Henry, pushing him away from the window.

"*Henry! Do as I say!*" she hissed. "*Go get both guns NOW!*"

Without hesitation Henry ran to the bedroom and scooped up the 30.06 and 12-gauge. When he returned, Inola looked very distraught and told him Nels was in great danger from the stranger. She quickly outlined a plan.

As Henry eased out the back, Inola moved down the front path, rifle in hand, to the dusty, widened area between the house and barns.

As young Henry approached the barn, he knew exactly where to go to see inside without being seen. A small, narrow calving door was away from the main room of the barn and he slid through it, carefully pulling the shotgun in behind him.

He could hear the men arguing as he crawled through the soft earth of the barn floor. He carefully stood up behind a short wall and saw his dad a few feet from the stranger, very angry and agitated.

As the argument grew more heated, the stranger steadily moved forward and suddenly lunged at Nels. Henry saw the flash of a knife blade as Nels sidestepped the thrust and, with a sweeping motion, grabbed a pitchfork.

With little space to maneuver, Nels blocked the attacks and held his own, but, with a barreling charge, the stranger knocked Nels to the ground. He lifted his knife and plunged it into Nels' shoulder. Henry tried to react, but knew if he fired the shotgun, his buckshot would hit his dad too.

He instinctively ran toward the fray just as he heard an explosion behind him. In slow motion he saw the stranger fall to the ground. He turned to see his stoic mother standing at the edge of the doorway, still cradling the smoking rifle.

The sheriff later ruled self-defense.

That day seemed to initiate a turning point in Nels' life. Even though his shoulder healed, his spirit didn't. His world turned dark, pulling him into long periods of isolation and gloom. He seldom laughed much after that, and as the months passed, Henry and Austin took on more responsibility for the ranch as Inola cared for Nels.

As he became more inactive, Nels seemed as if he resented the work of Henry and Austin, at times accusing them of taking over. His mind wasn't active in the work, so he never seemed able to remember things, and attempts to give back his responsibilities always ended in failure. They watched helplessly as he receded deeper into a state of isolation.

People assumed this behavior was a result of his traumatic experience and maybe that was so. As the months turned to years, Nels spent most of them in his rocking chair in a distant world of his own. Most people just thought he was growing old, but some whispered that he'd gone crazy.

At that time, in that place, a diagnosis of something more serious such as dementia was not in the realm of possibility.

By 1910, Henry had grown up fast. He was 24 and already recognized in the region as the head of Jensen Ranch. Austin had drifted off to Denver to find his way in the banking world, a place where he could escape farm labor and enjoy desk work and fine clothing. Henry had done a fine job of building the ranch into a solid business, not only because of his ambition but because he felt he had no choice in light of Nels' incapacity.

Inola continued her care of Nels, much as she had done for Bernard. It was backbreaking work for her to have to operate the ranch house and continue to care for Nels with his sometimes demanding, sometimes innocuous moods.

Yet, she watched proudly as Henry became the man that Nels had once been. He embodied her purpose and the key to their future. He was also at marrying age and she began to look for ways to encourage him to socialize more.

To the women of Rock Springs, Henry was *the* eligible bachelor. Ranching left little time for fun and relaxation, but Inola pushed Henry to get out and do other things. Saturday dances at the Grange were one of the few opportunities to meet people. A girl name Louise Simpson was usually there and became the primary reason Henry consented to go.

Sometimes Henry got to dance with Louise, but he didn't push himself further than that. Just when he'd work up the nerve to ask her again, another guy would sweep Louise into his arms and monopolize her the rest of the night. When that happened, Henry got so upset he wouldn't go back to the dances for several weeks.

Each week Louise looked for Henry and wondered why he'd stopped coming. Henry's excuse was that he had to take care of the ranch duties formerly done by his dad, and therefore he was too busy to take time out for the dances.

But never underestimate the power of a woman on a mission. With a little encouragement from her mother, Louise baked a cake and rode out to the ranch one day to see if it would find its way into Henry's heart.

When she arrived at the ranch, Henry was out in the field.

"Good morning Mrs. Jensen," Louise greeted her.

"Good morning! So happy you dropped by. Come in, come in!"

"Thanks. I thought I'd bring Henry this cake since he likes cakes so much."

Inola and Louise visited all afternoon and got to know each other. When Henry finally entered the ranch house at eight, Louise was long gone, so Inola presented the cake to him with a twinkle in her eye.

"You got a little gift today from Louise," she began.

"A gift?" How come?" his face reddening a bit with a little embarrassment. "She always teases me about how much I like cake."

"That's *so* nice," Inola said. She was laughing inside as she watched Henry in this moment.

"Now, be sure and thank her when you see her next time."

Inola took advantage of the opportunity to give plenty of advice on how to properly thank Louise.

Saturday night rolled around and Henry was a ball of nerves. He was glad Louise had shown interest, but he was also jumbled up inside about where to go next. In spite of Inola's coaching on the protocol to engage her in conversation, he realized he'd long since forgotten it.

When he made his way over to where Louise was standing, he said, "Hello," and "Thanks for the cake," but couldn't remember anything else he'd planned to say.

But Louise stepped forward with a big smile and said, "You're welcome, Henry" and didn't wait for a response. She simply took his hand and led him to the dance floor.

In the months to come, Nels' condition worsened, and his care required all of Inola's time. Henry helped by pouring himself into the work. But his thoughts were on Louise even though seeing her became more difficult.

Louise was determined to follow her heart and spent time with Inola on weekends, assisting her with housework or, whenever possible, riding along with Henry on treks to the far reaches of the ranch. When they were together, their

50

conversation was easier, mostly because of Louise's outgoing nature.

When Saturday nights rolled around, they not only danced but also fell into a routine of long walks on the roads around the Grange Hall, returning after dark just before the dance was done. Their friendship turned to love, and in 1913 Henry and Louise were talking of marriage.

Inola was excited at the prospect of having another woman on the ranch. Her long days in the house with a distant and silent Nels made time go by slowly. Inola began inviting Louise and her mother to the ranch house for coffee and wedding planning sessions.

A date was set for the wedding to be held at Louise's family home near Rockport. Henry and Louise also began planning to build a small cabin near the main ranch house, far enough away from it to be private, but close enough to the other buildings to efficiently operate the ranch.

Nels fell into a semi-conscious state, just weeks before the wedding. The family gathered one morning after Inola found him struggling for breath. As they waited just a few short minutes, Nels slipped away, ending his long journey from Norway to the fulfillment of his beloved dream.

As the wedding day approached and work on the cabin was finishing up, both Henry and Louise were busy with last details. As friends and family descended on the Simpson place, everyone felt a sense of joy that Henry and Louise were a match made in heaven.

Life in the cabin for the newlyweds was spirited and fun

and eventually settled down to the business of everyday life on the ranch. Henry busied himself with building up the herd, and Louise had her intentions set on building one of her own. A few months after the wedding she announced that she was expecting her first child.

The Jensen Ranch was again alive with happy activity and proved to be the perfect place for a new baby. The ranch had played such a big role in the Jensen family history and the arrival of the next generation was a significant milestone.

But, with the new comes the passing of the old. Grandma Inola gradually declined and passed away later that same year. Everyone was glad she got to see their new baby girl that would take her place in the next generation.

I was that baby and they named me Laura.

4
LAURA

It was uncharacteristically hot in June of 1931, but every day was going to be hot that summer. I was 16 and walking down the driveway without a hat. As I walked along, I watched my dog, Tallie, chase a grasshopper and I remember feeling that life was free and wonderful.

Summers were fun except for the times when Mama Louise insisted on making a farm slave out of me. First thing each morning I had to do house cleaning, dishes or pick vegetables. Sometimes she'd ask me to stay around and do whatever it is people do to vegetables after they're picked.

This morning I suspected Mama had arranged a date for me with a large tub of peas. That always meant work! I had to wash them and then—the fun part—squeeze the steamed pods to scare out the peas. Mama or I would cull and measure them to fill small canning jars.

Sometimes I slipped out the front walk to escape work. I was always careful not to let the gate squeak and alert Mama. I stayed behind the wagon shed and then hurried on for about a hundred feet to the back of the barn.

That day my horse looked up and I spoke to him softly in order to keep him quiet. I didn't need him giving my position away with a tell-tale whinny.

From there I stepped onto the road where I could claim I was out of hearing range if anyone called out to me.

Finally! I was free for my walk. Not a long one—just some time to be on my own and breathe in some fresh air. I wasn't really avoiding Mama because I didn't like her. I did. And what's more, I always enjoyed the time we spent together.

Mama was known as Lu because that's the nickname everybody gave her. She was a vibrant, adventure-loving pioneer woman who had learned to be happy in spite of her modest surroundings. She was tall and slender with olive skin. The chores she assigned to me weren't all that hard either. It's just that the world beyond the ranch seemed to be opening up for me, and in every way, I was blossoming! I needed a little time to dream alone.

Growing up on a ranch as an only child was fun except for the times I felt so far from everything. Especially summers when my school friends weren't around and life moved so slow.

Our ranch was forty-five miles outside of Rock Springs. It was one section of 640 acres, and people knew us for the spring wildflowers that grew on the roadside. Starting at the highway, they lined the entry to our ranch and surrounded the JENSEN RANCH gateposts. Flowers lined the whole driveway to the ranch house too. People always stopped and snapped pictures of their kids standing in the flowers. Invariably, they yielded to temptation and picked an armful of them.

From time to time Mama would remind me of our family's history at Jensen Ranch. She would say, "Laura, remember, your daddy was born just before Grandpa Nels and Grandma Inola got this ranch! He's stayed here his *whole life* and after we married he built our little house on a corner of the ranch. After Grandpa and Grandma were gone, your daddy took over the whole operation and we moved into the big ranch house where we live now." That had been the way it was all the time I was growing up. We had a long and rich heritage there at the ranch we cherished.

One day, in that June of 1931, I heard that Daddy was hiring summer help. He was hoping to get a good alfalfa feed crop that year, and the weather was cooperating so far. With thirty or forty calves born in the winter, the steers were fattened up by fall, ready for sale or butchering. The beef was divided up, some for our family to eat through the winter, some to sell to friends and some to sell at auction.

Thinking of who the summer workers might be was exciting for me! We had lots of boys at school, church and Grange dances, but I hadn't really taken them too seriously. But that day I hoped that whoever was hired would be *cute*!

At that time around Rock Springs, most of the boys were kind of rural—to my way of thinking. Even though I guess *I* was actually rural too, but some of the boys weren't particularly careful about their appearance or aroma, so that sort of eliminated a lot of them for me. Since The Saturday Night Bath was customary, by Friday it wasn't very fun to sit next to the boys in class who worked in the muck yard outside the dairy barns. Mama Lu insisted I take *two* baths each week, and she kept my dresses stylish and my hair combed nice.

When the day came for the summer help to arrive, I saw a truck turn into the driveway. I was walking along the road, so I stepped to the opposite side to avoid the coming dust cloud from the truck as my dog, Tallie, barked in excitement.

It was an old Ford, rattling and rumbling as it closed the gap between us. As it passed, the driver waved and I saw two cute boys seated in the back. They were dressed in a way that meant they were there to work. I saw them smile when they saw me and I was real excited to see it was true—they *were* the ones I'd hoped for! I didn't want to be obvious so I waited until the dust settled before I turned around and headed to the house.

It had happened so fast that I was caught wondering what to do next. The idea of having those two on the ranch all summer got all jumbled up in my head, and I couldn't decide if I should go directly into the house or stay outside and greet them. I decided I should stay and greet them.

I reached the house just as the driver parked in front of the gate. He got out and lit a cigarette. I smiled at him and said, "Hello, welcome to Jensen Ranch!"

"Howdy. I'm lookin' for Henry," he said.

"That's my dad, and I think he's out on the west side. He should be back any minute. I think he just went out to change the pasture site for the steers."

The two boys in the back of the truck stood, stretched and then jumped out. They landed right next to me and, boy, did I feel awkward! I said "Hello," and both boys nodded.

The tall one spoke first.

"I'm C.J. and this is Tom," he said politely. I was caught off guard again as I reached out to meet C.J.'s handshake. I remember his very deep-set eyes.

"Oh, here comes Daddy now!"

Daddy's truck barged into the scene and he hopped out almost before it had stopped rolling. He first looked at me and asked that I go into the house and get something to drink for the boys. Having covered that, he turned to the man.

"Hello, George! Thanks for deliverin' my crew here!"

"Well, that's all right. Just work 'em hard! Keeps 'em out of mischief, you know. Seems like a fair enough day, I guess...what time you figger they'll be done?"

"Oh, I can work 'em till dark, I 'spose. There's plenty to do around here right now," Henry said.

"Good. See you then!" George climbed back into his truck. As I walked into the house, I found Mama finishing up the dishes.

"Hi, Mama. Daddy wants some lemonade for the men."

"Okay. Good morning sweetie! I didn't hear you go out. So, I guess you've already met them?"

"Yes, the tall one there is C.J. and the other is Tom," I said as Mama peeked through the window. I got the glasses from the cupboard and watched as the boys talked to Daddy. I asked Mama what she thought they would be doing. I was hoping she would shed a little light on how the summer might play out.

"Well, your dad needs help with the hay, so I assume they'll be doing some of that."

I knew a little about hay season. When the workload was

heavy, and hay needed to be picked up before rain came, Daddy would sometimes ask me to drive the hay wagon. I secretly hoped that might happen this time. If it didn't, I thought I'd drop some hints about being free to help.

I didn't know it then, but the day I met Tom and C.J., I met two lifetime friends. Years later my life would be wrapped around them.

My folks worked from daylight to dark. I was an early riser and I liked to help Daddy hook up the team and get the equipment ready for the day's work. I preferred field work more than housework whenever I had the choice. The work days were really long and Daddy was a hard worker.

He always managed to keep things running smoothly and efficiently on the ranch. My little plan to get to know C.J. and Tom went well. I was a free spirit, and I knew they thought I was attractive, so being together was a bright spot in the long, hot days for them.

Sometimes I rode my horse to the work site. Tallie was never far behind. I'd named my horse Tanner, and as I rode out to the field, I was happy for my two faithful friends. Tallie, an Australian Shepherd, was black with white markings and one telltale white eye often found in the breed. He had been around for several years and I sort of inherited him from Daddy. Tanner was a red-colored bay that had retired from heavier ranch duties and I had also claimed him for my own.

I found the boys ready to gather the freshly-cut and drying hay. I hobbled Tanner nearby and climbed onto the seat of the hay wagon. The drill was to have the boys rake up the hay and pitch-fork it over their heads into the wagon. As the wagon filled, it was my job to call to the team and move the wagon forward, little by little, to stay ahead of the loaders.

I liked to sing softly to Bolo and Reggo, our big old team horses. Singing seemed to make our days go quicker. I sang the songs Mama taught me—some were silly and some were love songs, depending on how I felt that day. C.J. often sang along, but Tom rarely did. He could be coaxed into singing only if the rendition was really funny or loud.

By mid-summer the three of us had become good friends. Each of us had grown into roles that suited us— Tom was the serious one and C.J. was the funny one. I was the center of it all. Midweek was the day to break from routine and go to town for supplies. I made the household list with Mama Lu, and the boys, now residents of our old cabin, met with Daddy to create his supplies list.

When C.J. and Tom met our family, it was a new experience for them both. C.J. wasn't accustomed to work and he hadn't planned to meet someone like me. I guess I was different from the girls he'd met through flirty relationships. When we began working, I think he felt attracted to me. C.J. called me L.J., for Laura Jensen, and we really were kindred spirits.

Our summer days were filled with hard work, but our evenings were spent on the front porch, settled into low-slung willow chairs and watching fireflies as well as the fluttering moths that were drawn to the porch lights.

Tom liked to read and usually smoked his pipe and read while C.J. and I played guitars. C.J. was from a musical family

59

that performed on weekends in a band called The Wanderers.

The time spent on the porch after work days gave me a chance to compose verses that actually turned into keepers! C.J. added impromptu melodies so evenings were a time to relax and sing them in our willow chairs.

One evening we sang a song we'd made up on the hay wagon. I was watching C.J.'s eyes as we sang the new song, and in the fading light, with his face silhouetted by the sunset, I realized I was in love.

When we finished singing, C.J. took my hand and said we should go for a walk. Walking in the twilight, I realized again that C.J. was more than a friend. I sang a new song I'd just written and C.J. joined in harmony.

I wandered down a winding path
No destination in mind,
I didn't know what life would bring
What kind of things I'd find.

> *Then there was you*
> *So beautiful,*
> *Then there was you*
> *So lovely,*
> *There was you…*
> *There was you…*
> *Always you.*

When we finished singing the song, C.J. kissed me. That was my first kiss. I was kind of nervous, enjoying the moment but also thinking about how much we could be together in the days ahead.

"What are you going to do after hay season?" I asked.

"Not sure... you got any offers?"

"Well," I said. "I kind of think we make some great music together. Do you think your folks would ever consider adding an outsider to The Wanderers? Wouldn't that be great?"

C.J. thought a minute and said it might work. He told me later that he was not thinking about the music as much as the idea that a steady commitment would damage his flirting reputation!

We agreed to take some time to see how things went. We had to first prove to his folks, Daddy Bob and Harriet, that we were serious about each other and then see how things developed. I saw more of his family when he came to pick me up at the ranch to go to his house. I started traveling with their band on weekends, just helping out and spending time with Harriet. The Wanderers first announced me as a new member in the fall that year. I was just 16 and I immediately felt like a real part of the band.

I kept my grades up and was able to travel on Saturdays to sing—and to see C.J. For the next year, it was really an exciting adventure for us, because we performed my song as the closing act. It became a popular song at our performances and people always requested it in advance.

Despite C.J.'s reputation as a flirt, he treated me well. But old habits are hard to break, and I sensed something was wrong. It started in Boulder when a girl named Betty, who'd dated C.J. before, came to the dance. Boulder was a popular town for the band, and C.J. had quite a reputation with the

Boulder girls.

This night he pretended to be occupied with equipment setup as Betty and some girls came by to flirt, expecting him to fall all over them. Finally, things became awkward, and C.J. was forced to introduce me to the Boulder beauties, emphasizing that I was a gifted *singer*.

But the girls plowed right on ahead with their flirting. Boy, I was mad! But I kept my cool, knowing that I needed to give C.J. a little credit for trying to get through it.

Three weeks after the Boulder concert, Daddy, Mama and I made a trip to Boulder for ranch business. We were in the truck, making stops at the Feed and Grain, Western gear store and the Cattleman's Restaurant.

As we finished up dinner and headed west on Stoneway Street, we stopped at the light. Next to us was a car full of rowdy teenagers, and, when I looked, one of the guys called out to me. I didn't recognize him, but I saw C.J. in the back seat locked in a warm embrace with that girl named Betty.

At first I froze and couldn't talk, and as we drove home, Mama noticed I was quiet and in tears. I told her what I'd seen and she consoled me. Daddy just gripped the wheel and drove. I could tell he was really mad.

When we were back at the ranch, I remained in my room a lot that week, sorting out my feelings of betrayal. My memories of all the good times with C.J. seemed to fade in the sadness I felt for the way things had unfolded.

Later in the week, I talked to C.J. In spite of being caught red-handed, he was anxious to ask my forgiveness, but the irony of love and deception had hurt me too much. He begged, but pleading just made the situation worse. I finally realized that I could not trust him anymore and did what I knew I must. I broke up with him and also told his mom that I was quitting the band.

It was all a painful time in my life, but I determined that I would remain positive and focus on whatever lay ahead of me.

5
C.J.

Long before that fateful summer, C.J. had entered the world in 1916 as a smaller-than-average baby. His folks had picked Christian James as a name, but when his aunt took a first look at him, she called him "little Cutie-James," and ever since then, C.J. stuck. He was always a happy kid, bouncy, gregarious and fun-loving and kept everyone laughing.

With three older brothers, he was the baby of the family and seemed to receive the most attention. His dad was an easy-going man named Robert who was small and wiry. He didn't stay on any one job for too long, moving around to labor jobs that took him to various construction sites or road projects. Because he was an independent laborer, when jobs required him to travel a little too far he'd just quit and find something closer to home. Driving truck to the mines seemed to suit him well, but the constant job-shuffling mimicked the lifestyle of a gypsy.

C.J.'s mom, Harriett, was a large woman who loved to

eat during most of her waking hours. Standing beside her thin husband in family photos, they looked to be the perfect Jack Sprat couple. Harriett passed along her good nature to C.J., and together they kept home life upbeat and cheerful throughout his childhood.

His brothers were generally a picture of their dad, capable of work but not too serious about it. The result was a family that took life as it came with little planning or structure to their days.

The one exception was music. It occupied most of their time and attention and was probably the reason work was deemed a necessity, not a passion. Robert, or "Daddy Bob," was a natural at the guitar, and whenever he finished his after-dinner chores, he'd take it down from its honored position—hung on the wall by its neck strap—and begin playing.

As the boys drifted into the house for the evening they would find a corner and watch as Daddy Bob played and Mama Harriett joined him on the piano. In time, each of the boys found an instrument they liked—banjo, dobro, bass or guitar—and the family passed their time immersed in music.

By the time C.J. was thirteen he'd somewhat caught up in size and had the good looks and charm that made him the center of attention with the girls. He was thin-faced with dominant cheek bones, penetrating eyes and Elvis-style hair combed back on the sides.

When the family began performing their music in public, they made regular appearances at churches, Grange halls and school dances. People from miles around would come to relax with their families and socialize after a long week in isolated ranch houses.

The Wanderers gained a following that enabled them to supplement their income. C.J. loved the band because it seemed so adventurous and grown up to travel and perform. He had a natural talent for it and soon became the favorite of the crowds.

When they arrived at a venue, they'd set up and practice a few songs. C.J. learned to gravitate to wherever the girls were congregating, and in no time at all he'd charm his way into one of their hearts and spend the rest of the time talking to her.

One night in Hudson, C.J. saw his brother talking to an especially cute gal. He made his way over to them and joined right into the conversation. This annoyed his brother who wasn't at all interested in having C.J. around.

After a few minutes, C.J. simply asked the girl if she wanted to go for a walk and she eagerly said yes, because she was already hopelessly smitten. So, off they went, hand-in-hand while his dumfounded brother wandered back to the rest of the crowd.

This became C.J.'s trademark—no one could compete with his flirting. It created a lot of tension between the brothers on the ride back to Rock Springs.

The band became widely known in the area, and as the boys grew older, it became C.J.'s goal to have a girlfriend in every town. Not in a calculated way—he just loved being a flirt.

Once he'd met a girl at a dance he would stay in touch, writing mushy notes to her during the week. He charmed his way into her life without bothering to know who else laid claim on her. If ever confronted, C.J. was so quick-witted and fun that he was always able to land on his feet when things got a little tense. He'd become an expert at it because he'd practiced on his brothers for so long.

The small towns east of Denver made up the circuit for The Wanderers. The close proximity of towns provided a convenient network of families with cute girls. So a rivalry of sorts existed between C.J. and the boys from those towns.

Once, when C.J. befriended a girl in Moccasin, word got back to him that the local boys there were not happy about it. They considered it an insult for him to be raiding their little hometown brood. Although they didn't really have any claim on the girls, it caused a dent in their egos to think that outside guys were perceived as better than they were. In fact, they put out the word that they would rough up the brothers if they ever showed their faces in Moccasin again.

When The Wanderers were set to return to Moccasin, C.J. and his loyal brothers huddled beforehand to establish a backup plan if things got a little sticky. It was predictable that every guy and gal in Moccasin would show up for the dance and afterward make their way to a nearby lake to "watch the moon come up" (a.k.a. make out).

The brothers needed a way to somehow distract the locals so they could have a chance to steal the cutest girls. With a plan agreed upon, The Wanderers rolled into town that night, Daddy Bob and Mama in the truck with all the gear and the brothers in their shiny Ford sedan, ready to reel in the cute chicks of Moccasin, Colorado!

Sure enough, a gaggle of girls gathered near the stage as the band was setting up. "Part A" of the plan was for C.J. to talk the girls into joining them in a drive to the lake after the dance.

"Hi C.J.," one of the girls said, grinning as she stepped forward. "Nice to see you again."

"Well, if it isn't Colorado's most beautiful girls," C.J. said as he turned to face them and pour on the charm. "I think it's high time for us to share some quality time on a night like this. How's about if you gals be my guest after the show? I could probably talk my brothers into taking a little drive up to the lake if you'd like."

What C.J. didn't mention is that he'd *already* talked his brothers into it.

"Surrre, that sounds fun!" the girls said in unison.

"Now, here's the deal. This has to be a secret because as soon as the last song is played, we have to sneak out to our Ford near the road and get out of town fast …okay?"

"Part B" centered on the usual protocol of a mid-dance break when the emcee made a few announcements and the band members had the opportunity to use the outhouse. This night the boys talked the announcer into declaring that there would be a special presentation right after the last song. He invited everyone to remain for a few minutes for this prestigious ceremony.

The boys had also talked Daddy Bob into packing up their equipment for them after the dance. Daddy Bob agreed because he remembered what it was like to be a boy.

During the break the brothers ducked out to the parking lot and lifted the hoods on the local boys' cars, unhooking the solenoid on the engines' electrical systems. It was an old trick, but a harmless way to temporarily prevent the engine from starting. It would give the brothers a needed head start.

69

Right on cue, the band played a foot-stomping song to end the dance. As the boys took a bow, they waved a grand goodbye and stepped behind the curtain. Without missing a beat, they slipped out the back door as the announcer called for *"a great big Moccasin applause for... The Wawnnnderers!"*

As he began his build-up for the mysterious "presentation," the crowd stayed in place and waited in rapt attention.

Out back, on a fast run, the boys met up with the girls near the road.

"Hey! You made it!" C.J. said as he found the girls. They were giggling as they all piled into the Ford and tore up the gravel, heading for the lake.

Meanwhile, the confused announcer could find no one who knew anything about a presentation. He finally gave up and said goodnight to the crowd. The local boys smelled a rat and ran to their cars only to find them difficult to start.

Instead of going to the lake, the brothers found a back road that led to a hilltop overlooking Moccasin. They proceeded to get to know the girls a little better. They were also able to see the headlights of the cars driven by the incensed local boys who were racing at top speed for the lake.

The adventures of The Wanderers continued until C.J. graduated from high school. He considered accepting a few offers he'd been given to play for other bands, but The Wanderers needed his talent and he felt an obligation to his parents to stay on.

During that period Daddy Bob was still working as a respected tradesman. Although he didn't have trouble finding work, he was aging to a point that extensive traveling, combined with his work as a heavy laborer, began to take a toll on his health. He was asked in mid-February to be foreman on a large silo project just outside of Farmington, a small town twenty-five miles from Rock Springs. The commute created a hectic balancing act in order to make band appearances on Saturday night, stay in Farmington all week and then meet the band at the next gig the following Saturday.

The construction of the 40-foot silo had been nearly completed by May when the accident happened. After working on a complex scaffolding system to top it out, Daddy Bob had completed his day's work and was cleaning up the area at the base of the silo.

A board slipped off the top of the scaffold and fell, hitting him on the arm with a glancing blow and shredded the skin on his arm from bicep to hand. Had he been hit on the head, the force would have killed him.

He recovered okay, but not enough to continue his guitar playing. After some thought, he decided to think about retiring from working and performing.

In spite of his laid-back upbringing, C.J. had a resolve about advancing his music career. When he was apart from me, C.J. filled his days practicing, writing and moving about in the Denver area's music world. He was becoming well networked in music circles and focused on ladder-climbing.

After a concert in Highline, he met a man who was destined to change his career. Bob Bowman was an executive in a Denver talent company, and C.J. was introduced to him by an influential man who had heard The Wanderers many times. One afternoon during a practice session, the phone rang.

"C.J., this is Bob Bowman from Moondance Productions. I've got an offer I'd like to make you. I've heard you and your family were quite a band."

"Well thank you, Mr. Bowman. We were pretty blessed for sure!" C.J. said as he excitedly waved to his brothers to quiet down a bit.

"I'd like you take a little time to consider some music opportunities in Nashville. I can hook you up with some guys that would be a great chance for you to give your career a boost."

C.J. was stunned by his good fortune.

"I sure do appreciate the offer Mr. Bowman. I will definitely give it some thought and see what the rest of my family thinks."

As he lay in bed that night, thoughts flooded his mind about the ramifications of moving to Tennessee and leaving everything and everyone he knew.

Sleep escaped him and the next morning he tried to talk to his family about it. He wished he could find peace after each conflicting bit of advice came from them. But as fate would have it, he was about to have even more confusion in his life.

Rounding a corner one day in Rock Springs, C.J. came face-to-face with me.

"C.J.! How *are* you?" I said as I spontaneously gave him a hug.

"Fine! That's amazing! I was just thinking about you this

week!"

"I heard your band had broken up and I wondered what you'll be doing."

C.J. slowed his pace as he thought about an answer to my question. "Well, I know a guy in Denver who offered to hook me up with people in Nashville, but I've got to decide if I want to live that far away."

"I think you have a really *great* future in music, C.J.," I said, but immediately wondered why I'd just endorsed the idea of him leaving. I still cared for him despite our painful breakup and wondered if we had a future together. Could it all fit together? The two of us, music and a job that could earn us enough money to live an exciting life?

We talked, and before we knew it an hour had passed. We agreed to stay in touch and I walked away with a sense of happiness I hadn't felt in a while.

Just before Christmas, I followed through and called C.J. to say that I was coming to town the following week.

"Hi C.J. I'm calling to let you know I'm going to be in town next week. Do you think we could get together?" I asked.

"Sounds great," C.J. said. "It'll be great to spend some time together!"

On the appointed day, I was ecstatic as Daddy and I left the ranch for the hour-long trip to town. Daddy seemed quiet for part of the trip, but as we neared our destination, he asked, "Where do ya think your plans with C.J. are headed? You thinkin' of gettin' back together with him?"

I studied my father's face and thought about my answer carefully.

"Well, I still care about him, and I think he feels the same," I offered. "I don't know where his work with music is leading, but I'm okay with it."

"Are ya willin' to follow that life, wherever it leads?" he asked. I sensed his hesitation about C.J., and my voice took on a tone of defensiveness.

"Sure, I know he'll always make me a part of his plans."

"Well, I hope you're right, hon. My guess is you'll be always competin' with his music, so as long as you're okay with that…"

As we rolled into town, Daddy parked at the grocery store and I said I would meet him in an hour. As I headed down Main Street, I turned north and headed to C.J.'s house. I thought of how glad he'd be to see me.

The house was old, small and partially hidden behind bushes within a small picket fence. I passed through the gate and tapped on the weathered door.

"Oh, hello, Laura," Harriet greeted me as she opened the door. "What a surprise! How *are* you?"

"I'm well," I replied. "I called C.J. about coming by today. Did he tell you?"

"No…?"

I said nothing, all the while attempting to cover my disappointment.

"C.J. left for Nashville yesterday. I thought he'd told you. He was offered a spot in a band there and decided it was something he just couldn't pass up."

"Oh, I'm sure he is very excited about that, I said, trying to control the flood of emotions I felt. I thanked her, and as we chatted, I desperately looked for a way to leave.

"Well… I'd better run. My dad is waiting for me."

"Goodbye sweetie. I'll tell C.J. you stopped by!"

On the walk back to find Daddy, my tears came surging out from feelings of betrayal and lost love. I found a bench in front of Benson's Hardware. Although I sat in the sun, I didn't feel its warmth. I didn't care who saw me or what I was going to do next. The more I thought about C.J., the more difficult it was to accept the fact that he had deceived me twice. I knew it was going to be a lonely Christmas.

Daddy's suspicions had been right.

6
TOM

If there ever was a more opposite family dynamic than C.J.'s, it was Tom Sanders'. His parents, John and Mary Beth, were the epitome of regimen. They expected Tom and his older brother Tyrone to contribute to their share of the farm work.

Their heritage was British. The culture at home exuded proper sensibilities that bordered on stoicism. Although John seemed properly versed in intellectual things, he worked as a railroad man and had the necessary skills to succeed at farming. By the time Tyrone and Tom were in middle school, they were able assistants in most work projects with their dad.

Although Tom was reserved, Tyrone was decidedly quiet and rarely showed enough emotion for anyone to know how he was feeling about anything. The boys didn't complain about their heavy workload because it grew out of an unspoken expectation from John that everyone was to take care of things around the farm. They just accepted their life as young working men and left little time for foolishness.

Mary Beth was a tiny thing and sharply contrasted with six-foot-four John. They made an interesting couple. She was a meek and pleasant woman not prone to socializing, choosing only to keep her house in order and dutifully serve on the women's auxiliary at the Methodist Church. She loved the delicate aspects of decorating, and her exquisite taste afforded their home an orderly and pleasant appearance.

John had left England at age thirty-four and landed in Canada to begin a new life. His work as a draftsman was a foundation for his hope of becoming an architect. He met and married Florence Tonnagan and together they set up housekeeping in Toronto.

Their lives were just settling into a routine when she contracted smallpox and died shortly after Christmas that same year. John's work had advanced enough to demand his attention for long work hours, so he sent for his sister in London to come and maintain his housekeeping. As fate would have it, his sister had only worked for him a few months when she also contracted small pox and died.

John considered all that had transpired and knew he needed a fresh start. He moved to Denver and gave up on his dream of architecture. He found employment as a railroad worker, first as a yardman and then a brakeman. Two years after arriving, he met Mary Beth and they married in 1912. Tyrone and Tom were born shortly thereafter.

Tom was strong-boned and of average height, and while he might not have been known as a heartthrob, he was solidly built and good-looking in his own way. The Sanders' lives were a blend of stylish grace and the rugged, rural Colorado lifestyle. The boys loved to roam the countryside whenever time away from chores allowed, often hunting birds and small game. They considered each hunting success an indication of superiority over the other in a fierce sibling competition.

As a teenager, Tom joined 4H and did well, undoubtedly from his well-established work ethic. He generally raised calves and sold them at the county fair. Tyrone was prone to long periods of silence and loved to spend time alone in the open spaces around the farm. Hunting provided an abundance of time for this, and he often did it with or without Tom.

One October, Tyrone decided to go on an overnight hunting and camping excursion, and since Tom had evening chores, Tyrone asked Tom to join him the following morning.

At daylight, Tom made his way to the agreed-upon site and discovered Tyrone in his camp, dead in his bedclothes. The doctor later determined the cause of death to be heart failure.

This event was the most difficult for Mary Beth, who suffered in silence as was the usual way of handling her feelings. Tom made it through the school year and then decided to go to work the next summer to find a new pathway in his life. He befriended C.J. at school, primarily because of his easygoing, upbeat personality, which Tom found healing.

Just before school was out Tom told C.J. about wanting to find summer work. C.J. said he knew of work available at a ranch and, after asking around, connected with the right men to get hired. The year was 1931 and the boys spent their first summer on our ranch where they found more than work.

Their lives both changed when they met me!

The following year C.J. left for Nashville, and it was the last I ever saw of him. He wrote once, but only explained that he was on a new life path with no mention of continuing our relationship. The next few weeks weighed heavily on me. I stayed at the ranch and talked through it with Mama.

Tom returned the next summer to work for Daddy. He'd suffered through his grief from Tyrone's death, and I was feeling better after accepting the fact that C.J. was gone.

It was a bit awkward for both of us at first. But when we realized that we were both hurting, we spent time talking it through.

I appreciated the fact that Tom seemed to understand my heart. Compared to C.J.'s forward manner, Tom seemed laid back, and over time I began to fully realize the value in that.

Tom also found himself becoming a more confident friend and he valued the time he and I could talk through our difficult losses. He had worked there for four years, and we became closer friends, driving together to weekend dances in our old Ford.

Over the summer months, the long drives gave us more time to talk. We joked about never having to find a date. Daddy had taken a liking to Tom as well, and treated him like a son—partly because they were two of a kind, both hard-working, no-nonsense ranchers. By the end of that season, the conversation turned to how Tom could take a more active role in the future development of the ranch.

A plan came together in a most unexpected way, I'm

told. In the summer of 1934, Daddy was busy oiling the hay mower in the barn and looked up as Tom arrived one morning.

"I been thinkin'. I got an idea for ya' to chew on," Daddy began. "I got 640 acres and I sure don't want to keep workin' it forever. There's a natural divide on the east part of the ranch. I think it could be sectioned off to be its own outfit." He paused before continuing. "I think you could make a go of it if you wanted to."

He watched Tom as he spoke. Tom didn't say anything, but looked off to the horizon, just taking time to think about Daddy's idea.

"What kind of deal do you think it would take to get something like that going?" Tom finally asked.

Henry laughed. "Well, for starters," he said, "if you asked my daughter to marry you, it would speed things up considerable!"

Tom didn't react outwardly, but felt the blood drain clear down to his boots.

"Well…" he tried to begin but the words were lost in his throat. "I mean…that's awful nice of you to mention it. Truth is, I *was* thinking about asking her sometime."

Henry's face erupted into a wide smile. "Yeee-haw! Good *boy*!" He danced a little jig, and Tom was afraid he'd trip over the mower's sickle bar. Even Tallie barked at all the excitement.

"So here's what we do," Henry hurried on. "If you 'n' Laura *do* talk it over 'n' she says 'yes,' I'll give you two the land—no strings attached. But you can't tell her 'bout this deal before she says 'yes.' You can work the land 'n' live there, or you can sell it and keep the profits. Lu and I are hopin' ta sell our piece sometime 'n' take life a little easier anyhow. This'll give ya a head start!"

"Let me work this land thing out in my mind, Mr. Jensen. I haven't even talked about marriage with Laura yet, and I don't want to get the cart before the horse, if you know what I mean."

Saturday night arrived, and I asked Tom if he was going to the Rock Springs Grange dance.

"Sure, I've got a couple of things to finish up in the barn, so let's leave at seven," he replied.

I was excited for a ride to the dance and was ready and waiting at seven. I was also wondering about my own feelings—if it meant more to me than just another night at the Grange. Tom's steady friendship was beginning to feel like more than that, and I was cautiously allowing myself to think about whether I was in love.

As I jumped into the Ford that evening, Tom smiled. Getting to sit close to him in the narrow cab made it an even more beautiful drive in the warm evening breeze. The sights and smells of the open fields were mixed with the sweet smell of my perfume.

I felt close to Tom, and I think I eased a little closer to him than usual. There was a trust between us that I'd not experienced with C.J. As we talked, we shared our hopes and dreams, our feelings about relationships and I finally opened up about my disappointment with how C.J. had deceived me.

"The most important thing I want in a relationship is honesty," I said, and Tom agreed. As we continued to talk, we realized we were already near Rock Springs. Tom suddenly slowed and took a turn onto a gravel road that stretched toward a ridge of hills a mile west of the highway.

"Where are you going?" I asked. The sudden turn had caught me off guard.

"I have something I want to show you before we head into town."

"…Show me what?"

"Ain't tellin'" Tom smirked.

"Is it big or little?" I asked, watching his face.

"Both."

I could only offer a wry smile, but nothing more. Circling to the back side of the hill, Tom pulled the Ford to the edge of a high cliff in time to see the sun sinking into the horizon. I reacted to the scene with amazement: "Isn't it beautiful?"

Tom was quiet for a moment.

"Well, now you've seen the big surprise, want to see the little one?"

"Yes! What is it?" Tom reached into his coat pocket, and as he pulled his hand out, it was closed. I responded to his teasing and pried his hand open. He didn't resist. When I saw the ring I gasped.

Tom was smiling, and his eyes met mine as he asked, "Laura, will you marry me?"

7
A LIFE TOGETHER

Mama and I spent two months planning the wedding which was to be held at the ranch. The day seemed to come quickly, and when it arrived, the wedding was simple but memorable, a truly beautiful scene arranged in the expansive backyard.

It was filled with wildflowers and streamers with an elegant rose trellis, built by Daddy, forming the backdrop for the ceremony. Every aspect of the ranch wedding was a fine combination of rustic warmth and country beauty. Our friends came from Rock Springs to share our special day.

Since I had never traveled too far from the ranch, Tom had taken time to plan a honeymoon beyond our surroundings. He'd saved money for some time, and following the wedding, we headed west, stopping first in Strasburg for our honeymoon night. Then it was on to Denver to stay at the Grand Rockies Hotel to spend a wonderful week exploring the city and cherishing our time together.

Tom conspired with his buddies to move the old Jensen cabin from its decades-old location onto the land Daddy had given us. After finding the perfect spot and creating a foundation from native stones, they cleaned it from top to bottom. It was soon transformed into another cozy, first home, just as Daddy and Mama had experienced.

Tom had been mentored in the trades, as most ranchers are. Daddy had taught him the art of building, wrangling cattle, fixing machinery and managing finances. These skills earned him respect in the region as the Jensen Ranch prospered. The ranch herds had doubled in size, and Tom continued to build corrals and outbuildings to handle the growth.

I guess I was content in my responsibilities of running the household. Tallie was great company, often curled in front of our fireplace. Tallie and I also enjoyed the chance to ride with Tom when he monitored the most distant pasture land.

In the spring of 1938 I awoke one morning feeling nauseated. I stayed in bed thinking it was the flu, but when the symptoms persisted each morning, I knew it was something more. I talked to Mama to be sure and was thrilled to realize that I was going to have a baby! I really looked forward to telling Tom and I carefully planned my announcement for after supper one evening.

"So how was your day?" I began.

"I spent it down at the creek section, fixing fences" Tom replied.

"How is the calving going? Are we going to have a good bunch of calves?"

"Ya, I think I'm going to have to build some of the corrals a little bigger just to keep up."

"Great! Oh, by the way, you may want to add on to the the cabin a little too! We're probably going to have more ranch hands around real soon."

Tom studied my face as my meaning sank in.

"Really? You're expecting?"

I just grinned and nodded affirmatively. We spent the evening talking excitedly about all that this new family member would do to change our lives.

The months passed quickly as I prepared for the baby. Tom doggedly worked long hours to stay ahead of the demands of the ranch. Summer lightning storms were more frequent, and as July turned into August, it was a constant guessing game to outsmart the weather.

Late one evening Tom had finished putting up the first cutting of hay, hoping to get it finished before a coming storm. As his work increased to more frequent daylight-to-dark marathons he was thankful to be done at 10:00 p.m.

The sky had darkened further that day, with threatening black clouds. The thunder soon echoed across the landscape and lightning followed all too close.

A giant pine, standing at the end of the hay fields, tempted fate. The lightning found it and split it from top to bottom in a tremendous crash. At that moment, Tom was in the barn, but he heard the sound in the distance as he watched the tree topple. He stood motionless for a moment, to see what would happen next, and then saw the smoke and flames flaring up from the ground.

In a flash, Tom re-saddled his horse and dumped a few empty grain bags into a rainwater barrel near him. Yanking them back out, he threw them on the horse and spurred it into motion, heading for the house.

"*Laura! Fire! Get help!*" I heard him yell. He didn't slow the horse, but held its forward momentum, racing to the fire. Tallie sensed the importance of all the excitement and sped ahead, regularly offering a reassuring bark.

I got my wits about me and looked outside and saw the fire about a half mile in the distance. Panic did its best to keep me frozen in place, but I fought it off and went to the phone to call Daddy and Mama.

Tom was at the mercy of his horse's sure footing as they raced ahead in the dark. He carefully paced himself, with what landmarks he could faintly see, avoiding fences that divided the acreage.

By now the fire was moving with the evening breezes, headed for the long, precious windrows of drying hay. Without help, Tom knew he was facing a challenge, but he slid from his horse in one motion and grabbed his supply of wet grain bags.

The fire spread in a wide pattern, fed by the long rows of hay. They made the battle front impossible to keep up with. Soon it was obvious that Tom could not contain it by trying to beat out the flames, and he instead ran ahead of the flames to scatter the fuel supply contained in the windrows.

Eventually the fire grew to several hundred feet wide and he was at a loss to contain it. The changing winds curled the fire into two fronts and formed two walls of fire that advanced toward the distant roadway.

Soon, Tom could hear the shouts of Daddy and others who'd come to help, but their help was too late to make a difference. Exhausted, Tom collapsed to the ground and tried to comprehend all that had happened so quickly. Looking around he realized that the dog was missing. He remembered Tallie had come with him to the fire. He called, but to no avail.

When Daddy and the others came, they followed the fire line and eventually discovered Tallie's charred form at the far end of the field. The opposing walls of fire had come together, trapping Tallie in the fast-moving inferno.

Later, Tom told me that as hard as it was to tell me about our loss of the hay crop, telling me about Tallie was even harder. He had been a faithful friend to us for years, and Tom knew losing him would be crushing. When I saw him through the darkness, I ran to him, just glad that he was safe. But I knew from his tired and worried look that he was bearing a heavy burden.

"Laura, Tallie somehow got trapped in the fire and he's gone" Tom began carefully. I was stunned and took a moment to comprehend it all.

"Oh, Tom! That's terrible!" was all I could say. "I am going to miss him so very much!"

In spite of the loss, I knew deep inside that we were lucky the house hadn't burned, and we held each other as we grieved.

Daddy and the men brought Tallie's body to us, and as Tom dug a small grave behind the house, I gathered some of the native stones around the yard, and ringed the site with them and placed an old collar inside the circle.

In the weeks ahead, we assessed our losses which were about 80 acres of the winter feed crop. It took a big toll on the herd's feed supply and we knew how badly the affects would be felt. In spite of the progress we'd made in expanding the herd, we had to sell several head to try and compensate for our loss of several tons of feed hay.

In the midst of the sad days after the fire, the arrival of little Davey a few weeks later eased the pain of our losses. He was a big baby, taking after his dad, and he brought a lot of joy to the ranch. We were cooped up in the snug cabin for the winter so I had plenty of time to talk to him, make clothes for his tiny wardrobe and watch him discover the outdoors when the time came to emerge from the cabin in the spring.

It wasn't long before Lisa followed and we began to feel the pinch of how tight our small cabin was. Lisa was a little more of a handful than Davey and it accentuated our close quarters. As summer came Tom rigged up a little harness to tie Davey to the saddle and took him along on easy rides to inspect the herd. I couldn't resist taking a picture of them in their western outfits, especially the tiny cowboy hat Tom had found for Davey on one of our excursions to Rock Springs.

One evening as Tom settled around the fireplace, easing off his boots and releasing a long sigh of exhaustion, we began to talk about the increasing workload Tom faced and the questionable prospects for making ends meet. It was then that he shared with me his thoughts about moving to a smaller spread—one that would allow us to reduce our work and actually see fiscal daylight.

"Laura," he said, "I've always thought about Longmont as a great place to live. There are many more chances for finding a place with water and I think we could have enough cash from selling this place, we would be settin' pretty well for a change.

"I understand," I said. "But I don't think I could leave the ranch as long as the folks are still around."

I knew that he understood that also, and we dropped the subject for awhile. As I visited Daddy and Mama in the following months, I couldn't help feeling a little guilty about the relationship between their welfare and our moving plans. Both of them had slowed considerably, and Daddy was not doing much in the way of ranch development. He was simply hanging on because the ranch was all he had ever known.

Mama looked tired, and rightly so. She had singlehandedly cooked and cleaned and faithfully cared for the rest of us all of her life.

In 1941 Mama awoke one morning and discovered Daddy had quietly passed away in the night. She spent some of the time in silence and some in talking to him, thanking him for being at her side for all those years—26 to be exact. She knew the rigors of ranch life had taken a toll on him and he was simply worn out.

As she tried to comprehend all that this event would change in her life, her sorrow overtook her and she sat in her rocker, allowing her tears to flow.

We buried Daddy on the ranch, next to his folks' graves and not far from old Bernard Goertzen's grave site.

Part Two

MARK RELATES THE STORY
OF HIS OWN LIFE

8
MARK

Henry and Louise Jensen, my grandparents, had spent their lives on the ranch and worked it into a stable and profitable enterprise. Dad and Mom had done their part too, but they knew the time for change had come. It wasn't long until we Sanders left the ranch and moved to Longmont, Colorado, a few years after Grandma Lu had passed away and just after I was born. Since the rest of our life story is firsthand to me, I will take my turn as the narrator.

Longmont was west of Rock Springs about 120 miles, and my dad, Tom, liked the idea of getting out of the high desert's sandy soil. After the tough years, he'd decided to sell the portion of the ranch land that Grandpa Henry had given them, and he and my mom, Laura, set out to start fresh in a place of their own choosing.

By then, little Davey was eight, Lisa was four and I was two, already bringing torment to their lives. The land we settled on outside of town was just 16 acres. It was small compared to the Jensen ranch but a lot more green and fertile. There was already a small house but no out-buildings.

"Do you think we can all fit into this dinky little house?"

Mom said with a laugh. Dad was circling the perimeter as if it were Jericho.

"I think it'll be tight, but if we can all survive till spring, we'll have enough good weather to add on to it."

Dad paid the man who owned the property and it was ours. True to his word, shortly after the winter snow melted enough to reveal dormant grass, he began building an addition.

Working alone, he added to the house room by room until it was large enough for five. After that, he built a barn and garage and small sheds and pens for the chickens and pigs. Essentially, it was a self-sufficient farm and the whole family worked to provide for our own needs.

Mom and Dad were middle class and respectable, taking part in 4H, the grange and church activities. Dad was a volunteer fireman, all-around craftsman, mill worker by day and small farm operator at night. He was the always-present, rock-solid protector and provider. Mom was still a vibrant country gal at heart, game for anything fun and creative. We were a close, Colorado farm family with three kids growing up in the '40s—what could be better?

The farm was only four miles from Longmont, and Mom made friends easily. Grandpa and Grandma Jensen had never been much for church-going, but in Longmont, Mom found new friends at the local Baptist church on the north edge of town.

Things took a turn one week in August when she was invited to a week-long series of meetings led by a traveling evangelist. On Sunday evening she listened intently as the speaker presented a message she had never heard before.

She realized that her desire to respond to it was strong and enthusiastically stepped forward during an invitation to commit her life to God.

As an upbeat, kind person, her new commitment easily reflected her value system and desire to use her gifts to serve others. From that day forward we spent our Sundays at church learning about God.

Dad, however, was used to the farmer's life and would never think of giving up his Sundays for church. He served in his own way and was known as a dependable man of his word who was also ready to give to others. While our family was happy, the subject of church was understood to be off limits with Dad.

His relationship with us kids was fairly business-like. Oh, he was nice enough, but the remnants of his British heritage were too strong for him be comfortable as a hugger.

I remember one uncomfortable time when he and I rode together to go shopping in town. We'd gone through the motions of getting settled into the seat, and pulling out of the driveway onto the highway, setting out for the journey ahead.

I was painfully aware that not much was being said. Finally, he'd venture out of the silence.

"I found an almost-new hammer beside the road this week."

"Oh, that's good. Are you going to keep it?"

"Ya. I'll keep it in the truck for a spare."

Once that exchange was done, there was a long drought in the conversation. I'm sure he was deep in thought, planning how to solve some problems related to the farm, but I remember curling my toes and cringing at the deafening silence. I simply couldn't think of anything to say. I mostly liked just being with him, watching how he worked to build our little Sanders family empire.

While he ruled the working world, Mom was director of all things family. By the time I was five, she had created many holiday traditions, and most of them involved our own projects. We were not "po' folks," but we seldom bought things that we could instead make ourselves.

Saturdays were designated for crafts. Lisa loved cutting out her custom-drawn paper dolls but I preferred projects that reflected the Old West.

Once I built a Popsicle stick cabin, which I later took to the garden plot and created a complete ranch. I used more Popsicle sticks for fences, and scratched roads and trails into the dirt. Then I scripted an outlaw raid and burned the whole thing down.

As art director, Mom taught us how to get the most out of celebrating holidays. At Halloween time, we cut silhouettes of quarter-moons, witches, black cats and jack-o-lanterns out of construction paper and taped them on our windows.

We exhumed the old decorations from a worn box in the attic and re-hung them annually. They gradually became black-faded-to-lavender and orange-faded-to-salmon, but we kept them because of tradition.

The tape was barely removed from the Halloween-themed windows when a round of Thanksgiving silhouettes took their place. By then, the single-paned glass was often frosty from the cold weather and the thaw/freeze cycle added interesting water stains to the faded art. But year after year they were hung until we were in high school.

When the winter snows came, Mom shared our excitement about the new, white landscape. Before bedtime we'd crowd around the kitchen window overlooking the barns and watch the blizzard snow swirling around them, making exciting new drifts to dream about exploring the next day. When the time came to go outside, we dug out our boots and found the mittens Mom had knitted for us.

Since polyester ski-jackets had yet to be invented, our solution was to bundle up *Christmas Story*-style with two pairs of mittens, wool socks, tall boots, long johns, jeans, more jeans, undershirt, shirt, heavy shirt, ear muffs and coat with a hood. Mom patiently bundled us up tight and followed us out to the porch where we grabbed our sleds and headed for the hills.

Two hours later she managed the same procedure in reverse, pulling off each item, shaking off the snow and ice and hanging them all above the wood stove to dry. The grand finale was cocoa and buttered toast, enjoyed with our feet propped on the open oven door. She stoked the wood stove and listened as we related all the details of our adventure on the hill.

I often think back and admire Mom for her ability to cook under abnormal conditions. Since Dad was doing all the construction himself, our house was in construction mode for awhile.

At one point we didn't have refrigeration, but Colorado has seven months of natural refrigeration each year, so our food that needed freezing was simply stored outside in a wooden box, much like it was in the stories told about Great Grampa Nels.

Our plumbing wasn't hooked up yet, not so much because of the piping, but because our sewer didn't have anywhere to go until a septic tank could be installed. So one of my jobs was to empty what we called the slop bucket.

That was simply a bucket under the sink to catch the wet garbage that was then dumped out daily in the pig pen. In the Sanders home, I was appointed as the official Slop Bucket Emptier and Wood Box Filler. This explains why, in my adult years, I was even more motivated to choose a profession in art and design and not construction or farming.

On my eighth birthday, Mom threw a party and invited my friends from church and school. I still have a picture of us in the front yard, eating more-sugar-than-you-need sized pieces of white cake slathered with even more sugar frosting. We all have red Kool-aid moustaches and are decked out in our "good" clothes. "Good clothes" are casual but nice—classified somewhere between Sunday-best clothes and get-dirty-in-the-yard play clothes.

I remember that birthday as my favorite. Maybe I was old enough to see how much Mom worked all week to make everything nice for me. Or maybe it was because it was the birthday when I got my own bike. That summer Lisa had taught me to ride her bike, but, because it was a girl's bike with no upper rail and a tall seat, I could only stand on the pedals and ride without sitting.

My new bike was not new, just new to me. Dad had

found it in a second-hand store, and it was kind of tired looking. True to form, Dad had chosen it for its excellent mechanical condition and failed to see its overall tired appearance.

Even when I was only eight, Mom's tutoring in art registered with me, and I had a keen sense for visual and aesthetic things. It wasn't long after my birthday that I expressed an idea for improving my bike. Mom was all for it (I think she recognized Dad's oversight too) and the next time we drove to town she stopped at the hardware store and helped me pick out a pint of aqua-colored paint and some small brushes. I spent a few days working my magic, and I recall my sense of pride as I rode to school on a new-looking bike. I thought it deserved the admiration of the passing traffic as if it were a Rolls Royce.

There were things about Mom that we came to refer to as "classic Laura." Probably because she'd not driven much while growing up, she was directionally challenged. In time, she memorized routes to school and church and summer camp, but apart from that she had to work hard to find her directions.

That's not to say she wasn't smart and very efficient in other ways. By the time we were teenagers, the farm involved less of our attention. Our focus was on our high school activities, and Mom was our biggest sports fan— never missing a game. Dave was the athlete in the family, so high school sports were our default entertainment. Dad had a harder time going to games because milking time collided with the start times, but he came when he could.

Eventually, Dave graduated and left for the Army, Lisa

and I left for college, and we all met and married our loves. Mom and Dad began downsizing the farm and taking life a little easier. They were happy and enjoying life together, following their children's lives from a distance.

In September 1964 Mom and Dad celebrated their wedding anniversary. Lisa decorated the cake that said, "Tom and Laura 30 Years Together."

9
DARK DAYS

Eddie Payton was notorious in Longmont as a hell-raising drunk, and people made every attempt to avoid contact with him. At 23, he had either robbed, raped or beaten up anyone who had had the unfortunate experience of a run-in with him. His drinking habit started in high school and developed into a routine of such proportions that it dominated his entire life.

Eddie worked as a roofer during the day, but as soon as he finished work he headed for the Longmont Tavern, a less-than-respectable establishment on the south edge of town. The drinking crowd filtered in for Happy Hour and managed to entertain themselves with pool, storytelling or pinball machines until sometime around midnight, when they all called it a day and stumbled home.

The Longmont police all recognized Eddie's beat-up '53 Chevy and watched for it as a sure way to liven up their shift. They simply waited for the telltale signs of a car wandering out of its intended lane and confirmed it as Eddie's. More often than not, the cause for the wandering had started a few hours earlier.

Part of his routine was to get raging drunk, slam his

pool cue down and head for the restroom before leaving for home. Then he'd emerge, still fastening his pants, and bowl over a few stools as he found his way to the front door and eventually his car.

Once there, he'd gun the engine to its maximum RPM and tear out of the parking lot, peppering all the other cars with gravel. It was a wonder there was any gravel left on the lot. It was also a wonder that he had any friends left. But somehow he always made it home to his rough-and-tumble shack in the woods beyond the city limits.

In the late spring of 1965, Dad worked at a mill about ten miles from home. His previous job had been eliminated, and he'd faithfully worked the graveyard shift at this mill for five years. He was happy to be working and was able to juggle a little farm work around his night shift at the mill.

One morning in May he left work shortly after 2:00 a.m. and began his commute home. The route began in the high wooded areas and gently descended into the valley, crossing streams and low hills until reaching the farm lands.

This night, as his headlights lit the narrow Johnson Creek Bridge, he was already partly across when he saw the oncoming, speeding car barreling toward him. With no place to go, he was hit head-on by a '53 Chevy, said to be speeding at a hundred miles per hour. The impact sent Dad's truck off the bridge and into the rocky creek bed below. The following day a large photo on page one of the *Longmont Register* showed that there had been no possibility for Dad's survival.

I was 22 at the time, and Jamie and I were living in Orchard Heights, California. Lisa and Ron lived in Peru and Dave and his wife, Carla, in Alaska. When the Colorado State Police knocked on Mom's door at 4:00 a.m., she awoke and slowly realized there was someone at the door. She recognized the man as a police officer, but, in the darkness and confusion of the moment, things were jumbled and unclear to her.

"Mrs. Sanders?"

"Yes."

"Are you related to a Tom Sanders at this address?"

"Yes. He's my husband..."

"I'm Officer Bill Noland of the Colorado State Police. Mrs. Sanders, your husband was involved in a traffic accident earlier tonight, and I am sorry to tell you he is deceased."

Frozen in a state of shock, Mom simply listened.

"His body has been taken to the Longmont Mortuary, and you can contact them at this address. Do you have family here?"

"No... just the people at church."

"Here's my card if you need anything. We can direct you to some assistance if you need it. The mortuary will be open in a few hours, and they can help you with what you'll need to take care of."

As we gathered to remember Dad a few days later, we hadn't been able to wait for Lisa's delayed arrival from Peru. Mom was in a daze and feeling lost most of the time. She went through the motions, usually directed by Dave or me.

We stayed on in Longmont a few days and after Lisa arrived, we set about to make plans for Mom's future. We were thankful Dad had been a good provider. Everything on the farm was in good order, and with no farm animals, she could essentially live in the house with few responsibilities.

That traumatic event, like the one in Nels' life, was a defining moment that impacted her life from then on. In hindsight, it's easy to think of it as the worst thing she could have ever endured. But that gut punch kept us from realizing the second punch coming a few years later.

Mom lived on the farm alone, volunteering at church and doing housecleaning jobs to supplement her social security income. Since she'd been raised rural all of her life, she still had a toughened resilience. With the help of her neighbors and friends, she somehow survived the snow and icy roads of that first, long Colorado winter. But summers and winters came and went.

During the summer days she spent much of her time with friends at church and volunteered at summer camps whenever possible. But the long, dark winters were tough. Periods of depression set in, each one a little longer than the previous one in spite of the help others tried to give. She stayed home and struggled to find a sense of purpose.

"Hello, Laura?" the voice on the phone was tentative.

"Yes. Who's this?"

"This is Billie. Just wonderin' how you were doin'."

By that time, Mom was more withdrawn than people were used to.

"Oh, fine, I guess."

"What 'cha doin' today?"

"Not much. I'm just trying to decide what to do with some of the stuff I have. I don't want to get rid of it, but I probably should start thinking about it."

Thoughts clogged her mind and she ventured into a fog

of confusion.

"I don't have any idea what to do, and I just don't care. Why did Tom have to die? Why did he leave me here? Why don't the kids call? What am I going to do with this big place?"

"...Yep, I know that's hard, isn't it? Well...we're thinkin' about you and just checkin' in. Let us know if you need anything and hope to see you Sunday!"

People were kind in the present, but it didn't give Mom much hope for an uncertain future. I talked to her by phone, and we visited the farm when we could each year. By the time she was sixty-seven, I finally concluded she needed more help. It was just not feasible for her to remain saddled with the farm house as she faced her declining years.

We talked about moving her to Orchard Heights, closer to me and my family, even though it meant leaving her longtime friends. In our conversations, Mom was unsure from one month to the next.

At times, she was excited, but more often she was just not ready to make a decision. In the end, we came to a decision, about 40 percent her idea and 60 percent ours. We felt that once the change was made, she'd be okay with it. We began to realize that Mom's decisions were not the best, caused by her increasing periods of depression.

Moving day was set for August. We planned to drive out in June and begin scaling her possessions down. After that, we'd determine what would be moved. That year could best be described as "interesting."

I say that because it was an emotionally-charged process with no winners. Mom had her rights as an individual to live her life as she chose, but under this new paradigm I also had the responsibility to consider what was best in the bigger picture.

On one hand, I wanted to approach the situation with love and grace. On the other, I had a responsibility to complete it with business efficiency.

Had Mom been in a small house it might have been easier. But after forty years in the same big farm house, it was clear that downsizing was going to be painful. Adding to that, she'd always had the space to keep anything she wanted.

Some might describe her as a borderline hoarder, but not a shoulder-high-newspaper-tunnels-with-flattened-dead-cats-under-stacks-of-cardboard type of hoarder. She had nice enough things and preserved them well. But it was that other stuff, the odd choices made to save things that begged the question, "Why?" Those concerned me.

For years Mom had taught Sunday school. She was famous for the scenes from the Bible she created out of household items. They were artistic shadow-box creations of little houses, Ark of the Covenant fences and bath towel-draped people. This included a homemade concoction of plaster made from water, salt and soda, which did a pretty good job of imitating biblical architecture.

Toothpaste tube lids, matchsticks, cotton balls and random pieces of Styrofoam and cardboard were used to recreate many of the details of Old Testament life.

The big farm house was home to all of her project materials, tucked away in shoe boxes and envelopes. Living alone provided her an unlimited opportunity to stockpile all of it—pretty much as she darn-well pleased. Our plan was to have a garage sale in the spring and then a farm equipment auction followed by move-out in the fall.

Arriving at the ranch in Longmont that day in June 1982, I felt torn. I was doing what was needed, but I also felt I was the spoiler there to steal a treasure trove from Mom's castle. Through high school the house had been my home too, but now it had taken on a different persona.

What I saw then was somehow tinged with an old familiarity. The outside looked the same. I studied its grey cedar shake siding and green shingled roof. It was amazing that the asphalt shingles had any sand left on them after our childhood game of Annie Over, which involved bouncing a ball over the roof.

The lawn had its usual mix of grass interspersed with a variety of quasi-weeds and clover. The wooden front steps Dad had built forty years earlier were fashionably worn by thousands of encounters with work boots, Sunday-best shoes and harsh weather. They were the kind of boards that crafters would die for—rugged and rough-sawn, but gracefully smoothed over time.

For weeks we'd called Mom and suggested that she ready herself for sale day. But her mind was sidetracked after joining a knitting club with some girlfriends. This bright interlude was being interrupted by the unpleasant business at hand. My brother Dave and sister-in-law Carla flew down from Alaska to meet us there on what I jokingly called "pillaging day."

As Jamie and I arrived at the farm that day, preparing for cleanout, we sensed things didn't feel right.

"Uh ohhh..." I said with growing anxiety. "It doesn't look like *anything's* been done!"

Jamie agreed. I guess we shouldn't have been surprised, based on Mom's aversion to discard anything. I'd tried to give her the benefit of the doubt, hoping I would be proven wrong.

As we parked in the gravel next to the house, I saw the front door slowly open. Mom appeared behind the screen door, pausing there with a shy smile. It was evident that she was excited to see us, but her reserved side held her there.

"Well, hello!" she called out.

"Hi! How's it going?" we offered, half as a greeting and half as a veiled inquiry about the clean-up process. She walked outside then, her slightly crooked smile widening but still tempered by shyness. She looked older to me, but not old. Now, the waist-length hair that had been her trademark was gone—cut, home-curled and bouncing with a tousled look. Her gait had a hint of turned-in feet that presented itself more as timidity than physical defect.

In some respects she was a no-frills gal, but although her life was pragmatic, she had her own way with style. She maintained a simple but neat ensemble when going out for shopping or church, which was usually once a week. But her trademark look was a simple cotton "house dress," as we called it, often faded from age and innumerable washings.

"So how's the packing going?" I probed, all the while afraid to hear the answer.

"Oh, pretty good I guess," she chuckled. Jamie and I greeted her warmly and gave her a hug as we moved through the entry porch to the kitchen. The place looked very much

110

the same and a wave of nostalgia swept over me. Growing up, the kitchen had often doubled as a living room because the cozy wood-burning cooking stove was there, central to our activities.

As we wrestled our luggage through the kitchen to the spare bedroom, my suspicions were confirmed. Instead of a room full of boldly-labeled, neatly-taped boxes, there were two or three open boxes with their contents only partially disturbed. A smattering of clothing, dolls, knick-knacks and antiques were on the bed and floor, but nothing resembled readiness for a sale.

"So…," I began cautiously, fighting the urge to scold. "Have you been going through much stuff? I mean, how much is left to do?"

"Oh, I don't know… seems like I don't make much progress, I guess," she offered feebly. I glanced at Jamie and saw mild shock tainted with a hint of wry smile. The smile was partly from futility and partly because of hearing about Mom's "stuff" through the years. We'd come to expect not much would change and resorted to humor to stay positive.

I couldn't wait any more and headed for the attic. It was actually more than an attic—it was a full second floor with a bedroom and large storage room. Panic laced with frustration began to mount as I saw tons of stuff untouched: cans of nails sorted by size; envelopes of rubber bands; dozens of boxes of church bulletins with penciled notes written up, down and sideways on any open space.

There were boxes of old Christmas cards *and* their envelopes, one from her church friend that was half torn, and one faded envelope from some gal named Chris McKinney from ten years earlier.

This eclectic collection was what had eventually become known as Mom's "stuff." Stuff was differentiated from "things," such as furnishings or family memorabilia. Those were not what concerned me. It was all the time she'd spent on the stuff instead of preparation for a sale. It was the lack of a practical reason for keeping it all.

Armed with a full understanding of the situation, I grabbed a random bunch of papers and approached Mom. I tried to temper my tone and control my rising blood pressure.

"How are we going to be ready for a garage sale in two days if we keep stuff like this?" I pressed.

No answer.

"Why are we keeping stuff like ripped, empty envelopes? Who's Chris McKinney? I asked, holding it up as a visual aid.

"Well, what's it to you?" she responded defensively. "Just a friend…"

"I'm sure she's a great friend. I just don't see why it's necessary to hang on to it."

She looked at me blankly, as if deciding whether to respond.

"We're going to have to get busy and really move on this," I said emphatically, unable to quell my exasperation.

Finally, she answered, with indignation. "Well, I don't *want* to get rid of any of that stuff. That's *my* stuff!

"But you *just. Can't. Keep it!*" I fired back. I realized I'd already lost my cool in the first five minutes, but it was too late to retreat.

"We can't be moving all this to a smaller place. It just isn't going to *fit* anywhere!"

112

"Well then... I guess I'll just stay here."

That brief exchange was indicative of things to come. I didn't realize it at the time, but her statement was my introduction to the difficult task of turning one lifestyle into a new one. It also characterized the simple, skewed logic of early stages of dementia.

Some folks might think it sounds normal for that stage of life—or a justified push-back to an invasion of privacy. Maybe it was, but I found that it did parallel the degenerative pattern of behavior that developed in the years to come.

She was capable of making good decisions, but when feeling badgered or facing a challenge, she clearly retreated to safer, but illogical behavior. It was a tiny first step down a long road of our battles between her willpower and her welfare.

As we plowed through the process, Mom kept searching for ideas on how to avoid actually getting rid of anything. On a few occasions, there were items that she felt were too nice to sell, but all the while knowing she couldn't keep them.

"What do you want to do with your good dishes?"

"Well...I was going to give those to Carla."

Hearing this, Carla froze, knowing that she was cornered. They just not something she needed or wanted.

"I really appreciate that, but I don't really need another set...maybe there's someone else here in town that would like them" she proposed. She considered keeping them for the sake of being helpful, but there was a history of Mom giving away things and then unceremoniously taking them back.

In spite of these delays, somehow we managed to get

things ready for the sale on Friday. We got up very early, trying to stay ahead of the hardcore garage-salers who trickled in while we were setting things up in the yard.

That Friday morning was the toughest part of the job. It wasn't hard because of the buyers. It was hard because *Mom* was difficult to work around. She intercepted us as we brought items from the house. She circulated amongst the shoppers, grabbing things off the table. She took items back into the house—at one point arguing with a customer, "I need that back, it's not for sale!"

"But…it has a price sticker on it…"

Sometimes even though she'd decided to relinquish an item, it was perceived to be priced "too cheap." Besides the stereotypical garage sale items, there were also some strange ones we weren't too sure about displaying. One was a bed pan with a questionable heritage. It stood out, blazing-white against a grass-green backdrop, as if shouting, "Buy me! I'm disgusting!"

Midway through the sale the bed pan remained un-chosen. I think it was probably regressing into a no-one-loves-me complex, when a man stepped up and asked Jamie, "Apart from the obvious, what else could I use this for?"

"Oh, I don't know…" she stalled, "Maybe you could use it as a planter."

With a twinkle in his eyes he said, "Okay! Maybe I could put my *Pee-onies* in it?"

Overall, we thought things went well, under the circumstances, and by Saturday night we'd accomplished most of what we'd set out to do. But there remained a problem. The upstairs area was still full of those unsellable items—the miscellaneous papers and worn out stuff. Not just *some* stuff. A *lot* of stuff.

For the previous few days we'd danced around the little hissy fits that erupted any time we'd touch certain items in the upstairs piles of "stuff." It was soon apparent that Mom was incapable of understanding the concept of downsizing.

Jamie, Dave and Carla were in no mood to have a dog in this fight, so I stepped forward as the spokesperson for us all.

"Why are we keeping this?" I asked, poking at a teetering box of cracked doll heads.

"Because I want to *keep* that stuff!"

The hackles rose on the back of my neck and anything resembling a truce was now off the table. It had been three days since we'd started, and I'd reached the end of my patience. Sunday was bearing down on us and we were leaving for California on Monday. Without her cooperation we couldn't accomplish anything.

After several unsuccessful attempts at progress we decided that the only way we were going to wrap things up was to employ a little creative intervention.

The four of us quickly huddled and agreed on a plan of bait and switch. We introduced the plan by offering the bait to Mom in the form of a thank you for all of her work.

"How about if you take a break and go to church while the rest of us stay behind and clean up?" we proposed, cheerfully.

It was hard for me to be deceptive, yet deception with the goal of caring seemed to be a legitimate tactic under the circumstances. The stakes were high, the seconds passed—the moment as tense as a jury vote about to be revealed.

Surprisingly, her answer was yes, and, as she drove away, we danced and hugged before springing into action.

We began by swooping in with a neighbor's borrowed, open-box grain truck. We backed it up against the house and then gathered in the attic, grabbing armfuls of paper and flinging them out the window.

Two hours and a full truck of "stuff" later, we drove to the dump, knowing we'd done our difficult job, feeling extremely relieved.

The feeling of exhilaration was not that different from moments I remembered when finally getting our kids to sleep and then desperately fighting the urge to run out of the room before the little charmers woke up.

The atmosphere around the house had been tense all weekend, but we figured we were veterans, prepared to handle any fallout the moment Mom saw the empty attic. She returned and climbed the attic stairs as we braced ourselves. Fortunately, we were able to relax and the dialogue went surprisingly well.

Since there was nothing she could do about the situation, she chose to internalize it and became passive/aggressive, occasionally dinging us with little guilt darts for the next three years. Her summary assessment was always, "You'll probably throw *that* away too, like you did my *stuff*." It was a grieving process for Mom, but one that had to be experienced. When the weekend was done we all tried to move on.

It was my first experience at taking the reins of Mom's life. Little did I know what a ride it would be.

10
LIFE AT SUNRIDGE

We called it a trailer-house court, but "mobile home park" was the preferred name used by the 55+ folks at the Sunridge Mobile Home Park in the city of Orchard Heights. In a spirit of cooperation, we later upped the ante and called it The Sunridge Mobile *Estates* just to play along. Sunridge was a large, winding-street community with hundreds of well-kept units.

We found a brand new one that Mom picked out herself. The long U-Haul trip from Colorado had gone smoothly and Mom had done well, following the truck in her little green sedan. I'd talked some friends into helping us unload the truck and we eventually found a place to put everything.

Mom took to decorating her new home and added a little flower garden plot in front next to the street. We'd brought a wagon wheel signpost that Dad had made on the farm and replaced the old address with her new space number. The new digs seemed to give her a fresh energy and we were all happy that things had worked out.

After hanging pictures and moving in furniture, we shuffled things around to create a place to sleep that first week. Slowly she unpacked and we came to think of the 14 x 75 foot trailer as her home. It represented the sum total of her earthly goods. Sure, there was a small garden shed attached to her very own carport, but considering that she'd grown up in the wide open spaces of Colorado, it did seem very confined.

She ventured out to find the mailroom/garbage bin building and went on numerous walks to explore the maze of streets in the Sunridge empire. I did my best to watch things and make sure Mom was well cared for.

One evening as we walked down the winding streets, she blurted out a verse of a song, realizing it matched the moment.

> *"I wandered down a winding path*
> *No destination in mind*
> *I didn't know what life would bring*
> *What kind of things I'd find."*

Surprised, I turned to her and laughed, "Where'd you hear *that*?"

"Oh… When I was a girl my friend C.J. and I were just goofing off one day and made it up."

"I like it!" I said.

She smiled and sang a little more as we finished our walk and arrived at the trailer. I'd intended to ask her more about the song, but by then it was time for me to head home.

Things seemed to play out well in Orchard Heights. The biggest challenge for Mom was driving. After somehow passing the California driver's test she began taking ventures out for groceries. But it was a scary proposition for her. We drew simple maps and provided her with easy routes for shopping. Learning took awhile because for most of her married life she'd lived in Longmont, a town smaller than her new, adopted city. She'd traveled through the streets of Longmont mostly by rote memory, to and from shopping and church. But here there were freeways and more traffic to contend with.

For the first few weeks she rode to church with my in-laws. That helped her learn the basic distances and surroundings. When she finally drove solo, I would sometimes come upon her car puttering down the street ahead of me at sub-par speed. She had a little bobble-head lion with its feet glued to the rear window deck. It faced backward, always in a defensive stance as if to say, "Don't tailgate us or I'll bite you!"

Having Mom in the same town was a new experience for me. I was forty and had never lived near my folks after leaving home. By then we had two kids so "Grammie" was a fascinating new family member in their lives.

Besides family responsibilities, my business kept me busy working on the day-to-day things and managing growth. I guess that's my rationalization for not spending as much time with her as I could have. Her place was only a mile or two from ours, but visiting a small mobile home for more than an hour was not easy.

As the years went by, we changed churches and discovered a group called "Golden Agers" whose specialty was senior group travel excursions. Mom went on several of those trips over the years, to Washington, D.C. and sites in

Israel, Egypt and Greece.

I was so glad that she had the opportunity for a little fun and excitement in her life. She had a fun-loving side to her and was always ready for adventure. In Colorado, I don't think we went on more than two vacations, apart from holiday trips to visit relatives. Dad was saddled with the demanding schedule of morning and evening milking, and finding a substitute milker was next to impossible.

By now Mom had lived alone for more than a decade. We noticed signs of personality change but didn't think much of it. Mom had her own idea of how to do things. That gave an interesting spin with the Golden Agers who were seasoned tourists.

Her selection of luggage was our first clue, because for her it was not a Samsonite experience. She was not as concerned about how something looked as much as how easy it was to carry. Color-coordination was not involved in the process, and the ensemble was usually accompanied by an array of plastic bags.

One of Mom's perennial pastimes was photography. She had a simple Kodak "Brownie" camera for many years with a red, embossed plastic "Laura Sanders" ID label stuck to the top. One of her get-out-of-the-house highlights was to drive to town and pick up or deliver film. She burned through film like it was going out of style. The good news is that my childhood years are well documented.

"Line up for a photo, everyone!" she'd announce. Once in place we didn't have to say "cheese" because we were all smiling at her habit of bending over for a lower camera angle. After coming to expect this, my kids named it "the Grammie crouch." A least we had sunny blue skies behind us in most of the photos.

She also specialized in home movies. We recently digitized dozens of film rolls from her shooting days and got a fresh reminder of just how much action she'd captured. I guess I'd summarize her shooting style as a combination of still and moving photography.

She'd gotten so used to shooting on the fly with her trusted Brownie that she translated that technique to her movies. Sitting in a movie-night viewing session made your head spin. Ever the penny pincher, she didn't want to waste film, so each scene was only five seconds long before it jumped to the next one.

The effect was like being in a car at 80 miles an hour and seeing only a snippet before the next scene came into view. Come to think of it, we have a whole roll of that too, shot out the window of the car while she traveled through California.

Mom's life at the mobile estates went on uneventfully and we became accustomed to her routine and quirks. The trailer had a second bedroom that gradually filled up with "stuff."

On a couple of occasions I tried to suggest some organization just to class it up a bit. There was a desk, file cabinet and old sewing machine that, if arranged, could have a fighting chance at a nice layout, but the rest of the room held an increasing mix of papers and purchases with no place to go.

After awhile, I figured I'd just consider it a safe place to keep excess stuff and keep the door closed. The room finally became waist-high with stuff and un-navigable. On the farm, her stuff had always been there, but I wasn't around to see it change that much. Here, starting from scratch, it was apparent that there was a problem.

Mini stacks of papers or photo projects began to take up residence in the living room. Not too unusual at first— lots of people drag out projects and scatter papers around. But as time went on, the projects didn't go away. We noticed one day that we were stepping *over* things rather than around them. Then the kitchen counters filled up.

Since it came on gradually, we didn't think a lot about it. But eventually, the path from the front room to the back was bordered by rows of stacked papers. In the kitchen, the table was also stacked high and the kitchen counters were entirely covered with pots, pans and unrelated clutter.

If we asked about it, she was unable to tell us what the piles were for.

"What did you do today?"

"Oh….just going through papers," she'd say.

But she never had a sense of completion about any of it. Later we noticed that she seemed thinner and looked gaunt. As I visited, I would survey the kitchen and sneak a look into the refrigerator. I didn't see much in the way of healthy food.

One evening I found a pie pan that needed washing. I smiled as I remembered my childhood and Mom's pies. She was very good at making them, and my siblings and I were the grateful beneficiaries. I said, "Oh, did you have some pie this week?"

"Yes!" she said proudly, "I made it this morning."

"You mean you ate the *whole pie today*?!"

She looked sheepish and mumbled, "Well…yeah."

"What else did you eat?"

After a lengthy pause, paired with a far-off gaze, she said, "I can't remember… Nothing, I guess."

I didn't want to spoil our visit so I let it go. But about a month later we took her to Sunday dinner at the local "geriatric smorgasbord." We called it that because it was generally filled with senior citizens attracted to the all-you-can-eat-for-$7.95 fare. I think for some of them, it was their only decent meal each day, a pattern acknowledged by senior living experts.

As we filled our plates, we suggested healthy things for Mom to choose. But she passed on almost everything except dessert.

"Aren't you going to eat some healthy things?" Jamie asked.

"Yeah, I am—I'm having some pie!" she grinned.

"But having just pie isn't very healthy."

"Well….pie is good!"

We had a good laugh about it, and, ever since that time, it's been my mantra with Jamie to say "PIE IS GOOD!" anytime I feel like dessert.

As funny as that philosophy seemed, it raised red flags in our thinking. I was not even familiar with the word "dementia," so we just chalked up the bad diet to the quirks of getting old. But as Mom's health began to deteriorate, we wondered why.

The Sunridge gang had an all-court potluck every

Thursday night, so we were comforted by the fact that she got at least one good meal each week. She began to look forward to these events. After awhile she figured out that filling her pockets with dinner rolls before heading home supplemented her grocery budget. That theory advanced to chicken legs wrapped in napkins, cookies and more.

Most kids think some of the things their parents do are weird. My own kids tease me about some things, so it just seems to be a generational thing. But little by little I was conscious of the fact that Mom's actions were more than weird. People were starting to notice.

Looking back now, when it is easier to surmise that dementia was advancing, I can better understand it. We all establish living patterns and habits and make allowances for everyone else's behavior. In my case, I found myself becoming defensive anytime someone would chuckle about Mom's quirks. I rationalized that it wasn't as bad as people thought. Basically, I was in denial that something bigger could be happening. I wasn't even sure what it was.

Later, I began to resent the jokes people made about her behavior. I found myself protecting her weird lifestyle for no other reason than just an innate loyalty for who she was. She and I were very close growing up. She read the bedtime stories, taught me to cook, helped me learn to draw and was there to comfort me when I got bumps and bruises. Now, listening to people snicker at her unorthodox actions was painful to hear.

In time I realized that I couldn't "fix" things any more. As she moved deeper and deeper into this bizarre arena, I felt myself pulling back from defending her. I moved into a

124

season of denial, because I just couldn't, or wouldn't, handle it.

I realized I was moving more frequently to a "loving deception" defense by making excuses for her actions that I knew were not accurate. I loved her too much to admit the truth, but the guilt from the deception I was carrying was equally upsetting.

11
LIFE AT MILLWOOD

About 1995 we could see Mom's health declining. For several months we'd also become increasingly concerned about her driving habits. Even though she'd always been directionally challenged, she was getting more confused and wandering off familiar routes.

We were worried about her safety in driving and the danger of getting lost in a bad part of town. When I'd had a chance to ride with her or have her follow me to our house, she tended to drift all over the lane and drive too slowly for traffic.

No amount of hints or questions about quitting got anywhere. I was at a loss to know how to make any changes. Then one day intervention was again the key to success. Only this time I wasn't the one to initiate it.

Mom was having trouble swallowing and was diagnosed as having a constricted esophagus. Each time we were able to observe her at mealtime, she choked on her food. After a year of a doctor's attempts to temporarily stretch the esophagus with an expansion tube, he finally prescribed surgery. This would fix it permanently so she could eat without choking.

The appointment was set and we drove Mom to the hospital in Sacramento. After a morning of paperwork, well wishes and reassurances, she was off to surgery and before we knew it, she was done and resting in the recovery room.

That day was another benchmark in shaping Mom's life because it triggered several different things all in the space of a few short hours. Following surgery the doctor met with us and explained that things had gone as expected for the esophagus, but there were other concerns to discuss.

"Hello, I'm Dr. Sterner," the surgeon began. "During surgery we discovered that there is some severe liver damage. Are you aware of the cirrhosis? It is usually caused by hepatitis or a pattern of alcohol use."

Anyone who knew Mom knew she was an ardent teetotaler, so that option was off the table.

"Maybe we just missed those empties under the piles of paper," I joked.

(Note to self: not a good idea to joke with a surgeon about life issues.)

He just stared at me, so I thought it best to redirect my original approach.

"...No, we weren't aware of anything like that," I said.

"Well, I consider her condition serious and I cannot release her to live alone any more. I notice she seems relatively confused, and I don't think it's a good idea to place her in any risk."

Since Mom had traveled to Peru a couple of times, the hepatitis was possible but no outward signs of it had existed.

We were never able to determine a cause, but we had to accept the fact that it was serious.

Back home again, we moved her in with us for a few weeks until we could sort things out. During that time we took her to a follow-up appointment with her general practitioner, who was to share the final test conclusions.

The news was even worse than expected.

"Did the surgeon talk to you at all about the liver?" he inquired as Mom and I sat down on the tiny stools in the exam room.

"Yes, he said there was some… sore-osis or skurosis or something?" I replied.

"What we have is cirrhosis, but we haven't determined a cause. Bottom line—this is going to have some impact on her life expectancy."

I watched for Mom's reaction but there was none. Even though she was sitting there, her disconnected, placid look eventually communicated to the doctor and nurse that I was there to listen and speak on her behalf.

He continued, "I think you should get her into a care facility of some kind where they can monitor her health.

"What do you mean about 'the impact on her life expectancy'?" I pushed on.

He pointedly met my eyes as he answered, "I would say she has probably about six months to live."

The news hit hard and I struggled with my emotions as I tried to comprehend the ramifications.

"I've also noticed that her confusion seems to be more pronounced than I first thought. As we've watched her today, I've decided to recommend that you watch for signs of what appears to be dementia."

It was our first official introduction to the word. However, with the devastating prognosis of a six-month life expectancy, any focus on the dementia, which was still a foreign concept to us, was lost. Mom didn't seem to react at all to the news. She took it in stride, mostly because she was not grasping the ramifications.

The search for a care facility took top priority, but was not a difficult choice. Millwood Retirement Center was right down the road from Sunridge-ville and was a highly-regarded facility in our city. It was described as a continuing care facility.

That meant Mom could enter first into the independent living format starting with a one-bedroom/kitchenette apartment—something similar to what she was used to in her trailer but with the advantage of eating in a common dining hall. She could then move into a studio apartment—no kitchenette/bed in the living room. Then as the need advanced, she could go into another facility across the parking lot called an "assisted living center."

I had talked to caregivers and friends who faced eldercare decisions and learned that the most common question asked is "Which child will take care of the folks when The Time arrives?"

Without a plan, the process was not that different from playing "Old Maid." That's the card game where the object is to avoid getting stuck with the bad, Old Maid card. I've seen the eldercare game play out in the same way.

It routinely follows one of the following patterns: the

child who has the natural gift or inclination to do it steps forward; the child living closest to the folks is *assumed* to be in charge—even if this person may be the least suited for the task; or, no one steps forward and the parent suffers by bouncing around to foster or nursing care homes. Then a lingering guilt, accompanied by hard feelings, exists among the siblings for an indefinite period of time.

In my case, my brother lived in Alaska, my sister in Peru, and Mom and I lived about midway between them. So the handwriting on the wall was pretty clear: I was elected.

A few days after Jamie and I interviewed at Millwood, we were told an apartment had just become available. That was great news, but it meant I would again be broaching the subject with Mom about moving. That was the tough part—like "poking the tiger," as I called it. Prior to the surgery, we'd tested the waters about care facilities, but she'd been adamant about staying where she was.

Jamie and I huddled on several occasions that week, and I called my siblings, relying on their wisdom and intuition to decide just how best to proceed. Since Mom was in our home after the surgery it was easier to observe her. Some of the fight had gone out of her. It was apparent that she was confused more than we'd realized, and, with the dementia diagnosis, it was now more easily recognizable as that.

When the time came, I eased into the topic carefully, but I didn't word it as a democratic vote. It was more of an announcement of what was to come. Fortunately, I could blame the doctor for prescribing group living.

"Mom, your doctor has said that you can't live in your trailer anymore. Your liver is bad, and you need more assistance from someone who can help you cook and take care of your health."

She was watching me with a smile and a passive expression of cooperation.

"You mean not in my trailer?"

"Yes."

I didn't try and flood her with too much, too fast. I made sure I paced the information according to her response.

"Where would that be?"

"Well…we found a really nice place right down the street here, and you could have a nice room and wouldn't have to cook anymore."

"What about my car?"

"You can keep the car, but you probably don't need to drive too much now that you don't have to shop for groceries." I carefully continued in a level and moving pace, clearing the path ahead for each baby step of progress.

"We can go see it tomorrow if you want, and you'll see just how nice it is! Does that sound good?"

"Yeah, I think so. Would I keep my car?"

"Yes, there's a place to park right outside your place there," I said, reassuring her. The car topic was one she'd struggled with the most. Concern over limited mobility is common for people who face lifestyle changes.

The Millwood visit turned into a luncheon provided free for us and all went well. The staff treated her like royalty—welcoming her, introducing her and giving tours of the beautiful dining hall. Mom was smiling and a little overwhelmed by all of the attention.

And what a lovely meal!, we all thought. *This trumps the*

Senior Smorgie Joint any day!

So, since she was living in our home, the tricky transition of moving was made easier by the fact that she had been away from her home for over a month. The realities of her trailer were slightly removed in her thinking. That situation was my best ally because it allowed me to carry out the move without her going through a lot of emotional stress during her post-surgery recovery.

I again found myself knee deep into the task of moving her possessions. The amount of furniture and belongings was not as daunting this time, but I still ended up hauling a couple of trailer loads to the dump before moving the rest to Millwood.

Mom had saved the usual—hundreds of news clippings on a variety of subjects. She even liked to take pictures of her television screen: here's Billy Graham in Atlanta and one of the President speaking before Congress. Here's one of a two-headed calf.

I saved many items and tried to box them into a collection that she could cherish but still keep manageable. Her friends had been faithful in sending her notes and cards, and I especially wanted to keep those intact. Her friend Francis had remembered Mom's birthday every year since she'd arrived in Longmont. There were sympathy cards from Dad's funeral too, and as I read them, I again experienced the loss Mom had endured.

"Laura, you are forever in our prayers."– Shelly Travers

"We are so saddened from Tom's sudden death and your loss."– Marla Folsom

"So sorry to hear the news of Tom's accident. I can't

imagine how awful that must be for you. - Chris McKinney

During the moving activities, we were cognizant of Mom's terminal prognosis. I called Dave and Lisa, and we agreed to begin plans for her final arrangements, ironically, while also working out *living* arrangements. It was quite a time of upheaval, and Lisa really wanted to come to the States to see Mom right away. She did not want a repeat of her experience of missing Dad's funeral.

We agreed she would fly home as soon as possible so she could talk to Mom before the darkness of memory loss closed in. Even so, when she arrived a couple of weeks later after traveling 4,000 miles, she was unprepared for what happened. Entering the apartment, Lisa excitedly said, "Hi, Momma!"

"Oh... Who are you?" was the reply.

Lisa stopped in her tracks. "I'm your daughter, Lisa..."

"Oh, my goodness! Hello!" Laura said, chuckling with embarrassment. She wanted a way to recover and cautiously looked at me to get her bearings.

"So how are you, Momma?" Lisa went on. "I hear you're feeling better!"

"Yeah, I guess..." Laura struggled to assemble her thoughts as did Lisa, who was reeling with emotion, trying to hold back tears and grasp the changes that had come on so quickly. Her last visit had been only four years before, but the changes seemed to have accelerated so rapidly.

The homecoming was a devastating experience for Lisa, and I finally realized just how things had changed. Dementia was now making an impact on more people than Jamie and me, and it was a steep learning curve for everyone.

The week flew by, and when it came time for Lisa to return to Peru, she understood very clearly that it would be her last time with Mom. There were tearful goodbyes and an admonition for me: "Take good care of Momma."

Then something incredible happened. What I thought to be possibly a few summer months together with Mom turned into late fall, and then spring. Mom surpassed her scripted time allotment and actually gained weight. She looked and felt better than ever.

I stayed in touch with Dave and Lisa, but all I could think to say was, "She's doing much better." It soon became apparent that her time would stretch far beyond the doctor's earlier prediction.

When Mom continued to heal and gain weight, the only challenges for me were managing her finances and her dementia. Her car had been parked in the lot at Millwood. The only driving she did was to the Senior Center to attend a three-dollar breakfast and dance on Wednesday mornings.

Her love of dancing, which began with Tom, never faded and she didn't miss an opportunity to dance. She became so confident in her driving that it was sometimes hard to know where she was at times. In August I was completely unprepared for where that would take us.

It began with a routine phone call to her room.

12
AN ADVENTURE

I forgot that it was Senior Center Breakfast and Dancing Day. When I called her room, she didn't answer, so I waited an hour and called again. Nothing. I still didn't worry until noon when I got a call from Jill, the front desk gal at Millwood.

"Did you take Laura out today?" came the question.

"No, not today."

"We were wondering earlier where she was, and, after checking, we noticed her car was gone."

I tried to think where she might be, but for the moment I couldn't come up with anything.

"Let me call you back. I'll do some more checking with her friends. If I can't get answers I'll come over," I said.

I got nowhere until I remembered her Wednesday dance excursions. It took awhile to find the Senior Center number and follow the voicemail options to their dining hall, but finally a shrill voice answered, "Good morning, Senior Center, this is Becky..."

"Hello! I'm trying to locate my mother, Laura Sanders, and I was wondering if anyone there saw her at the breakfast."

"Just a sec." The phone clunked down, and I could hear Becky call out to someone across the room.

"Anyone seen a Laura Sanders here today?"

After a muffled conversation, Becky came back on the phone. "I'll let you talk to Helen here. She knows her."

After a *long* pause, Helen made her grand entrance into my drama.

"Hello! This is Helen. Becky says you're looking for Laura?"

"Yes! She didn't return to Millwood Retirement Center this morning," I explained. "I was wondering if anyone saw her leave there."

"Well, I asked around and some of the other gals did. Said she mentioned going on a trip today. Something about going to see 'Tom?' They thought she must be going to see family or something."

"Ohhh, no." I groaned audibly.

"Anything wrong? Helen asked.

"Yes! I'll explain later," I said, quickly hanging up the phone and running to my car. When I arrived at Millwood my mind was racing and I felt the onset of panic. I knew she had a good three-hour jump on me.

"What'd you find out?" Jill asked as I entered the lobby.

"I think we're in trouble. It sounds like she's taken off for Colorado, thinking she can see Dad. Her mind is messed up, and I'm trying to figure out where to go from here. I think we should call the CHP and see if they know anything."

"Let me get you a phone book," Jill said.

After what seemed like an eternity, the phone answered at the California Highway Patrol office. I explained our dilemma and gave a description to the officer. He promised to investigate and get back to me.

An hour later, as we dealt with growing anxiety, Jill's phone rang. After a few moments of silence, she looked up at me and covered the mouthpiece on the phone.

"They say they did stop a car on highway 50 a little east of Sacramento a couple of hours ago. The officer involved stopped it for erratic driving behavior, but, after talking to the driver, he let it slide with a warning."

"May I talk with them?" I asked.

"Sure," Jill said, handing me the phone.

After supplying more details, the officer explained that the route was in a less-patrolled area, which would take some time, but promised to post an alert for the vehicle.

After calling my office, then Jamie, I said, "I think we need to go after her." She agreed and I raced home to pick her up. After throwing some of her things together, she was waiting for me as I drove up.

Highway 50 is a circuitous route and increasingly remote as it heads east to Lake Tahoe. We thought of worst-case scenarios if Mom ran out of gas in a god-forsaken area.

As darkness approached, I leaned on the gas pedal, and Jamie and I traded ideas to second-guess Mom's thought process. After a few exchanges, we realized it was ridiculous, because there was no logical thought process, considering Mom's current condition.

We decided to take highway 49 as a shortcut, figuring we could intersect with highway 50 near Placerville, a route Mom may not have thought to take. After driving for an hour, we made our way into South Lake Tahoe and continued on.

Another complication we faced was that we were now in Nevada and uncertain of how the transfer of jurisdiction would affect us. It was possible no one else was looking for her. By nightfall we were on a remote route, without many opportunities to stop and inquire. We knew continuing to drive was just a gamble, but what the heck—we were in Nevada, and gambling seemed appropriate.

Rounding a curve about 9:00 p.m., we neared Utah and stopped for gas at a small station/grocery store in the remote Nevada town of Eureka. I decided to call the number of the California Highway Patrol officer I'd spoken to earlier.

The voice at the other end brightened as I identified myself.

"Yes, we've been getting some cooperation from Nevada, and I have a number for you there." As I searched my pocket for a pencil, she read the number. I called it, and, after being transferred, I soon heard encouraging news.

"Hello, Mr. Sanders? This is Officer Williams of the Nevada Highway Patrol. We got word from the sheriff's office in Fallon that they located your mother just west of Reno. I have word that they've taken her to the Reno office."

"*Reno...?*" I asked incredulously.

As I listened, he explained that they'd found her at a gas station. After calling in, the officer with her made the identification based on the outstanding APB and detained her. She kept saying she was fine and on her way to see someone named Tom.

Amidst the relief that she was found, I was frustrated that we'd driven 200 miles too far and faced another 200-mile return trip. Jamie and I were totally exhausted and hungry, so we decided to take a timeout to eat.

Forty-five minutes later we were back on the road

140

with Jamie driving, headed for Reno. We arrived well after midnight and found her car outside the station, surrounded by several police cars. As we stepped inside, we were met by an officer of some sort. He must have seen the look on our faces and guessed our mission.

"Sanders?" he asked.

"Yes…Mark, and this is my wife, Jamie."

"Hello, I'm Lieutenant Wells. I guess you must be ready to get this over with. She seems fine other than not making too much sense sometimes."

"She has dementia. I'm just glad she's okay—I'm amazed she is," I said, more to myself than to Wells.

"Yeah, I guess she stopped for gas someplace near here, and the attendant said she didn't have enough money to pay the bill. She seemed pretty confused so he went ahead and called us."

"I'm just glad it worked out," I said.

"Follow me. She seems fine, like I said, and has a great appetite! She's eaten just about everything we can scrape together around here!"

We walked down a short hallway which opened into a large room scattered with desks and chairs. Off to the side, on a short couch, sat Mom, semi-dozing. I approached nonchalantly.

"Mom? …Hey, Mom! How are you doing?"

She looked up, nonplussed.

"Hey good lookin', whatcha got cookin?" she mumbled and grinned. It was her canned greeting, and she felt so witty remembering the words to that old song.

Jamie leaned in and gave her a one-sided hug. "We were

worried about you, Laura," she said.

"*Why*—what's all the fuss?"

"I guess we'd kind of like to know what *you're* doing *here*," I answered.

"Well, I want to visit Tom... isn't that *my* business?" she asked indignantly. She was a sight for sore eyes with her trademark knee-length aqua dress and worn white sweater peeking out of the navy trench coat she always wore. She still had a few stray curls bouncing over her forehead, which indicated she was fifteen hours late for getting her hair combed.

Although she was safe, I was still wrestling with three simultaneous emotions: upset at the seriousness of the danger she'd been in; sad because of her innocence about Dad being still alive; and my inherent sense of humor popping up about the comical scene in front of me: "This is Maxwell Smart, wrapping up a case here at the beautiful downtown Reno Police Headquarters..."

Mom seemed so very oblivious to what our concerns were—this was all so logical to her. I sat down on the couch close to her and put my arm around her shoulders and looked into the innocence of her eyes.

"Mama, it's not a good idea to drive all this way on your own, you know...?"

Her expression changed instantaneously from innocence to defensive frustration.

"Oh I been drivin' all my *life,*" she retorted. "*I* know what I'm doin!"

As gently as I could, I responded, "Mama, you know that Tom died a few years ago, don't you?"

142

"He di….?" She quickly caught herself as the sudden realization clicked on.

"…but it's really nice that you still love him. I know it's hard to remember all that."

Silence…count to five as she looked off into space…

"How about if we go and get some breakfast? Does that sound good?" I interjected. I'd learned from experience to use the Blindside Tactic to divert her confusion with a completely different, simple topic that would take her mind off the thing she was stuck on. I didn't want her to feel badgered when she didn't understand the seriousness of her actions.

"Ya! That's fine!…"

I was again amazed by how quickly a distinct change could take place in her mind. Her thoughts of visiting Dad were already forgotten.

Jamie took over the banter as I finished up the paperwork with the police. It wasn't long before we were at The Logger, a cozy log café, where we ordered chicken-fried steak and mashed potatoes. And pie. Hooray for pie!

As we finished, I loaded Mom into my car, just like I'd done at Tuesday Lunch, and Jamie followed us in Mom's little sedan. I couldn't help but wonder about this crazy adventure that had taken us all to a very out-of-the-way place. I was glad for a happy ending, but felt older and wiser about this game I had to play and the role I'd been given.

Two hours later we dropped her off at Millwood. I don't think she remembered anything at all about her original goal of taking a trip to see Dad. She just smiled and thanked us as if we'd treated her to a nice, long mid-week outing.

I guess in some respects, we had.

13
DEALING WITH DECEPTION

If there is one thing I've learned as an observer of dementia, it is that in a world of seemingly endless, painfully routine days, you can expect the unexpected. By visiting only weekly, seeing Mom's life play out was like watching a stop-action film that only shows every seventh frame of the scene.

I could easily sense the pace of her decline, but then things like the Reno Rendezvous occurred as a wild card that upset the predictable pattern.

Mom was blissfully content in the Millwood independent living apartment, still cheating death, a year after her predicted short life span.

One day I woke up to the fact that her finances were becoming an issue. We hadn't previously worried because of her prognosis, but when she surpassed that timeframe, with no end in sight, we needed a new game plan. The money she had socked away from the sale of the Longmont farm was being eaten up at the rate of 10 percent per month. I calculated that at that rate she could only cover about another six months of rent.

That fact smacked me squarely, and I had serious anxiety

about where it would lead us. As much as I appreciated Jamie's support, I knew there was no chance that she could ever endure the live-in, mother-in-law-with-dementia idea.

I sought advice from the Millwood staff and the California State Senior Services Agency. They both gave us good advice about taking a qualification test to apply for Medicaid. If we could prove that she was mentally disabled and her tax records could show her next-to-zero assets, then her living expenses would be covered by social services indefinitely.

The day of the test arrived. The visiting representative and Mom made themselves comfortable at the kitchen table while I looked on. I had no idea how long the test would take or if she would pass or fail.

Please, Lord, don't let her have some miraculous moment of brilliance right now!

"Laura, I'm Margaret Simpson from Senior Services, and I would like to ask you a couple of questions."

Mom looked flattered to have a new friend who was kind enough to be interested in her welfare.

"Okay," she smiled.

"What year were you born?"

"1916, I guess."

"What is the name of the president?"

"I don't know...Bush?... I guess. Bush?"

"Where do you live?"

"Right here."

"...No, I mean what's the name of the place where you live?"

"Let's see, I guess... Millwood Retirement Center?"

146

"What year is this now?"

"2000?"

Shoot! Just our luck she had to get them all right!

After that brief exchange, Margaret stood up. "Okay, thank you, Laura. It's been nice talking to you! I need to be on my way now so... you have a nice day, okay?"

I played the gracious host and walked her to the door. I was stunned that the test took less than five minutes. Stepping into the hallway, we walked together and Margaret said rather matter-of-factly, "I'll be submitting the paperwork to get this taken care of so you should be getting some forms to sign real soon. Can Laura sign okay?"

Oh my goodness! What does this mean...did she flunk or not?

"Yes. Are you saying she *will* or *won't* qualify for Medicaid?"

"Oh! Yes, she will. She failed our screening test. I do this test every week so I know the signs. Even though the answers may have been right, almost all of them were offered in the form of a question. There was enough confusion that says she shouldn't be living independently."

I couldn't ever *remember* when I'd been so happy about someone flunking a test! I almost hugged ol' Margaret! Sixty days later Medicaid was covering all of Mom's rent and would do so for the remainder of her life.

But there was one more aspect to this major development that needed to be dealt with. The ruling that she was unable to live independently meant Mom needed to transfer into the assisted living wing to qualify for aid.

It meant *moving* again! *Yikes!* The thought of seeing another moving van with six-inch letters promising

"ADVENTURE IN MOVING" petrified me. I'd had enough adventure already.

Three weeks later a room opened up (that's the public relations way of saying someone else's loved one just died). So we headed into move number four. Add to that the fact that Jamie and I, in the past two years, had also moved *her* mom, aunt, uncle and stepfather. It would be safe to say we were feeling like we were experts in geriatric care.

Most people struggle with downsizing from a large place to a small place. But for older people it is intensified by an awareness that their lives, in general, are shutting down. They won't accept the fact that 2,500 sq. ft. of stuff can't fit into a 900 sq. ft. space without a tiny bit of compromise.

On the plus side, Mom's new room at the assisted living facility was nicer than her independent living apartment. Having cleared the moving and financial hurdles, we were feeling pretty good about her new situation. Mom liked it also.

The only thing I felt worse about was that the atmosphere in the dining hall was pretty sobering. She'd come from a dining hall where the excited buzz at mealtime was like eating on a cruise ship. Now she was eating with others who wore bibs in suffocating silence, shattered only by the ear-piercing greetings of the overly-upbeat staff members who'd chirp, "How we doin', Mrs. Sanders? Are we going to eat our Jell-o today?"

The reply was usually one of silence. Mom didn't seem to notice the downturn in her peers' demeanor and actually loved the attention from the staff. She was now the young, vibrant one. That struck me funny since she'd been deemed older and less capable among the independent gang across the street.

In a few weeks I noticed that the switch to new digs seemed to introduce new patterns of behavior. Lurking somewhere in Mom's memory were those Bible-scene shadow boxes she'd made for teaching Sunday School, and apparently she was still on the lookout for construction materials.

On one occasion when I joined her with my guest badge proudly displayed on my lapel, I entered the Joyful Memorial Dining Room and noticed she'd scooped up all the little empty creamer containers in sight. Not just hers, but her table-mates' as well. Back in her room, I would later find nested stacks of them in a drawer or under the bed. Unfortunately, so would the ants.

When it came to her penchant for collecting things, no amount of questioning, lecturing or chiding would convince her to stop. The score was Housecleaning Staff: 0, Ants: 5. And silly me, I was slow on the uptake and didn't realize it was only the third inning.

Why stop with creamer containers when "her" silverware was there for the taking? Forks were her favorite, and when I'd check her room later, I'd find them in what I began calling her loot drawer. Each week I'd return a handful of them to the dish room.

There was a very large common lounge with cozy fireplace just outside the dining hall. Mom liked to sit out there during the day because it provided a lot more interesting things to observe than did her room. In fact, she was there so much, she soon adopted the main couch and declared it hers.

One day, as I entered the building, I saw front-desk Jill looking into the lounge area. I looked too and caught Mom in a dispute with another lady.

"Laura claims that couch is hers and won't let anyone else sit there," Jill said with a smile. I was impressed by how calmly she explained the situation. The staff was always so great about how they dealt with Mom. They never made her feel like the full-on kleptomaniac she was becoming. When they would try and gently encourage Mom to share "her" couch, she responded by taking the couch's throw pillows back to her room.

For the next few months, whenever the couches looked bare, the housecleaning staff and I would faithfully retrieve anything from her room that didn't look native to its surroundings.

One thing I kept in mind—Mom wasn't incapacitated to the point that she couldn't carry on a nice conversation or make some good decisions. As long as my input provided most of the momentum, she would answer me and was fine to talk with.

She was almost always cheerful and, taken in context, I could have enjoyable visits. It's just that she couldn't generate too much understanding of a topic without prompting, and couldn't navigate beyond the anchor of her familiar surroundings and routine.

It was like hosting a visitor from a different state. If I were to talk about streets, parks and landmarks, the visitor would have a third-person concept of those places. If I drove them there, showed them each place, they could appreciate it far more. But if they were later asked to drive themselves there, their ability to do so would be limited.

As I thought ahead to the prospect of a long stay at Millwood, I also had to come to terms with how I'd take on the larger role of overseeing the affairs of her life. Mom had always taught us to be truthful, and our family always held integrity as a valued character trait. That's why, when dementia came along, I had to come to terms with adopting a creative approach to truth.

When Mom's welfare was on the line, and she had no ability to make rational decisions, I had to make them for her. When something needed a solution, and she became obstinate or combative, I felt I had to use more "loving deception" to handle things. I justified it by saying that it was the dementia I was battling, not Mom.

It was counterintuitive to my value system to use deceit, but it was the only way I could help her (and keep my sanity). Even though the majority of times with her were good, the confrontational ones were draining and stressful for me.

Shortly after moving Mom into the assisted living wing, craftiness again seemed to be my best ally. Mom never drove her car anymore, yet she was very protective of the idea of keeping it. But the now infamous Reno Rendezvous forced the issue.

Each time we scaled down her living situation, there was less space for possessions. She seldom wanted to release anything, and, furthermore, she could recite the list of items that were in storage, even though it had been awhile since she'd seen some of them (no memory problems there)! She was adamant about not getting rid of her "stuff."

I kept the inventory list kind of hazy and close to my vest, and, as a result, was able to keep her calm about the state of her possessions.

When the day came to extricate the car from her grasp, I simply told the staff my plans and then drove it home. Eventually, I sold it to a friend, and later, when Mom asked about it, I simply said it was in storage. That seemed to satisfy her, and I breathed a sigh of relief. I noted the achievement as another item to be crossed off my list of eldercare hurdles.

Every time I thought we were cruising down life's straightaway, free from bumps and turns, something else came along to prove me wrong. One week when I was popping in for my Tuesday lunch date, I found Mom, with freshly coifed do, sitting in the lounge on "her" couch with a man.

Well, isn't that nice. She has a friend to talk to.

As I approached, I swung around to the front of them so as not to ambush them from the rear. In fairness to Mom's memory difficulties, I always began a conversation with an introduction of some sort so I could discreetly slip my identity into her mind and allow her the dignity of not having to admit she didn't recognize me.

"Hi, Mom! How's it going today?"

They both met my eye. I turned to the gentleman and said, "Hi, I'm Mark, Laura's son."

"Hello! My name is Richard."

"Nice to meet you, Richard."

I paused for a few seconds, just long enough for an uncomfortable silence. It was probably only uncomfortable for me, because time moved slower for them.

"Well, I just came to see if you wanted to go out to lunch, Mom."

"Of course!" she said, as we excused ourselves. A few visits later, over the course of the month, Richard seemed to be a fixture around Mom. Later, I saw hand-holding and puppy-love grins when I stepped into the room. When I asked Jill about this, she made no attempt to cover her smirk. "Yes, they seem to be a 'couple' now!"

What first seemed to be cute now took on a little deeper meaning. I told the family Mom had a boyfriend and most of them had a reaction of curiosity laced with humor. As her caregiver, I had to consider the ramifications of it all. I'd read about other seniors who married and had an immense amount of trouble with shared assets and rocky, family-blending experiences.

The friendship seemed to be going along steadily until suddenly I noticed Richard wasn't around anymore. When I asked Mom, she said she wasn't happy about the fact that he always wanted them to go to his room to hang out. I discussed this with Jill and she said, "Ah, yes, this is a fairly common phenomenon in senior care."

Couples from Mom's generation were increasingly setting aside their views on marriage and celibacy once their lifetime spouse was gone. On their next relationship they just went directly to fun and games. Fortunately, Mom had enough cognizance left to know the difference.

A few weeks later I still didn't see Richard around. I asked Mom about it again. She replied, "He doesn't come around anymore. All he wanted to do was go to his room and

I told him I didn't want to do that."

Later I told Jill, who responded with a grin and said not to worry.

"Laura has had others call on her."

"Really? You mean the couple from her church that visits her?" I asked.

"No, there was another man I haven't seen before. I just noticed him because he came to my desk asking for Laura. Since there is an open-door policy for the main lounge, I just went and got Laura from her room, and they chatted for a while in the lounge.

"I wonder who *that* could be. He didn't give a name?"

"I think he said… Nick or …maybe Chris. Something like that."

"Oh, yeah! I think I *do* remember a Chris in some of her Christmas cards one time. No, that doesn't make sense either because Chris is a woman.

But the thought stayed with me and later that month I went to Mom's room while she was in the salon with Alexis.

I found a rubber banded bundle of cards and quickly found the one in question. Chris McKinney, *that* was it! Even though I was curious about Chris, as the weeks went by, learning more about the connection took a back seat to other concerns.

14

DEMENTIA, DEPRESSION
AND DIFFICULT DAYS

By 1999 I felt I understood what it was to be a seasoned caregiver. But I could only claim to be son, friend and advocate on a personal basis. The real caregivers were the Millwood professionals who were with her day after day and night after night.

I was more like a stockholder who dropped by to confirm things from a bird's eye viewpoint. I was not there for the day-to-day issues dealing with diet, pharmaceuticals, incontinence, hygiene, house rules, federal law and the additional responsibility for all the other residents.

I've learned that many individuals with dementia experience alternating personality changes. They can be cheerful and cooperative for a year or so, and then change to a season of anger and belligerence.

My personal experience along those lines happened when I stopped by one Tuesday in June for our lunch date. I didn't find Mom on her fireplace lobby couch and wondered if her hair appointment was not quite finished.

As I peeked in, I saw someone else in the "let's make

you pretty" chair. When I asked Alexis about Mom, she said, with a pouty little expression, "We couldn't get her to come in for her appointment."

I thanked her and promised to check things out. Mom's door was always closed, so I gently knocked and then knocked again. I heard a muffled, "Who-izzit?" and I answered, "It's your son, Mark!"

After a minute the door opened just a crack, and I could see that even at noon, her room was dark. The black-out shades were down, and she wasn't wearing her glasses, indicating that she'd been asleep.

"Hi," I said.

"Mark…?"

"Yes, it's just little ol' me!"

She opened the door further and greeted me with a sheepish smile.

"What are ya' doin' sleepin' at this hour?" I said with a casualness that deflected my inclination to judge.

"I don't know. Let's see, what time *is* it?"

"It's noon, time for lunch! I thought I'd take you out if you're up for it."

"Oh… Okay!... I guess I could."

As she searched for her glasses I probed a bit.

"How come you wouldn't go to have your hair done?"

Immediately I saw a flash of anger appear in her eyes. "Oh, they tried to make me go down there, and I kept telling them my hair doesn't *need* fixing!"

"Well, it's free and it's good to keep up your style and grace, you know!"

"I don't think it's *good* to wash it all the time. It ruins my

156

hair!" she said with growing anxiety.

"Well, that's true to a point," I conceded for the sake of diplomacy. "But I think once a week would be fine."

"Well, I don't think it's good to *wash* it all the time. It's not good for my hair!" It was a repeat of verse one, with only the word emphasis slightly changed.

Time out. No use ruining a good lunch date!

"Well, let's go to lunch. I'm starved!" I said, using my patented Blindside Technique to calm her down.

Things went characteristically smoothly once the setting had changed. But each time I visited for several weeks after that, the situation reverted back to the same pattern. She'd retreat into depression and hole up in total darkness during the bright, sunny days outside.

When I arrived, I'd lightly tap on the door and then quietly open it, just so I could survey her condition firsthand. She'd often be lying on the bed, clothes on, with a light blanket pulled over her. As I routed her out of bed, I would sometimes pull up the shades and announce, "It's a gorgeous day out there! Why don't you pull these shades up?"

"Because *that man* is out there. I don't want him *lookin'* at me!"

"What man?"

After a few interview sessions, I was finally able to put together the facts. A man had been gardening one day (on his own property about 50 feet away) and she felt a strong paranoia about him being there, able to look into her window. That concept had stuck in her mind for weeks, and, in her depression, she had responded by pulling her blinds down.

As much as I tried to explain otherwise, I could not

get her to change, and I found the blinds down the whole summer. At some point that behavior pattern left, but as soon as it did, another took its place.

Mom had always been frugal, and during the winter months I found that it was very cold in her room. Not known for being shy, I would walk over and turn up the setting on the thermostat.

"Whataya' doin?" she'd bark.

"It's really cold in here, Mom. Don't you want to have some heat?"

"No! It's too expensive."

"Well, guess what? It's free now! …It comes with your rent! Yay!"

"No, it's *not!* I have to *pay* for that." She'd move in right behind me and turn it back down. I'd argue and turn it back up, and she, back down. On that particular day I was stressed out anyway, and as our time together ended, I turned toward the door and mumbled a goodbye. I felt tears sting my eyes as I realized how awful things had turned out for the bright, fun-loving mom I'd known for most of my life.

I paused in the hallway long enough to regain my composure before walking to the desk to talk to Jill. I encouraged her to see if the staff could help me. We ended up with a solution to turn the heat up when she was at lunch or even at night when she slept. But try as I might, I never did convince Mom that it made no difference on her monthly expenses.

Just like her inability to understand window paranoia and room temperature issues, she fell into a pattern of not

158

wanting to change her clothes. When we moved her into the assisted living unit, she had a six-foot wide closet that was packed with hanging dresses, skirts and sweaters. Boxes of personal items such as photo albums covered the floor of the closet.

I began to notice that on each Tuesday visit she was wearing the same old aqua-colored cotton dress and white sweater. I asked Jill about it and she said that in fact, she wore that outfit *every* day. Once again, I was unsuccessful in convincing her to wear something else. In our conversations, I would dig through her clothes and pull out something else to wear.

"That's too bright."

"That's too long."

"Not that old thing!"

Okay, not a tenth as old as that thing you're wearing.

This went on for almost three years; by that time the sweater sleeves had three-inch holes in the elbows. No crafty ideas of mine worked to change things. On occasion the staff could convince her to take the dress and sweater off if they promised to give them back after laundering in an hour or so.

But no matter how many times they laid out other outfits on the bed as a strong hint, she put the Aqua-Woman costume on again. When she sank deeper into a pattern of unreasonable behavior, and refused to disrobe for the staff, they backed off. Many were afraid of her. They took to stealing the dress and sweater after she went to sleep, washing them during the night and then sneaking them back to her room before she awoke in the morning.

During all of this, I had my own relational issues with her. Since I worked at an office job, I generally came in wearing slacks, dress shirt and tie. As I made my way over to the Laura Couch, more than once I heard the whispers (old people's whispers are not subtle).

"That's Laura's son."

Intellectually I understood it to be just casual chatter, but emotionally it generated guilt because I feared people thought I wasn't taking care of my mom who looked like a down-and-out, homeless woman.

As frustrating as it was, I came to accept the boundaries of just how much of her behavior I could control. It was futile (and unfair to her) to push things during her belligerent stages. Only once, before I understood how dementia works, did I get forceful in trying to change her will and I still regret it today.

It started one day when I noticed her nails were long. Not just a little long—approaching vampire status. When I casually asked why she didn't cut them, she retorted with strong resistance.

"I don't cut them on purpose! I *like* them long!"

"Mom, it's not healthy to leave them long. Here let me help you."

No! Yes. No! *Yes!* It usually took about fifteen minutes of negotiations and blindside attempts before I could convince her to let me cut them. Eventually I succeeded by making the stipulation, "We can't go to lunch until your nails are cut…" That usually worked, but only after repeating it several times.

But today it had been twenty minutes, and we were still arguing. Finally I decided to just make it happen and I

160

gripped her hand while trying to cut the nails. By then she'd lost about 40 lbs. and her arms were essentially bone with a thin layer of skin around them, almost like a broomstick wrapped in tissue paper.

In fighting back, she was amazingly strong and as we arm wrestled, I suddenly realized I would break her arm if things proceeded the way they were going. I simply stopped and pulled away.

Angry and fed up, I left her room, assuming she could eat in the dining hall, and frankly, not caring whether she ate at all. As I reached the door, I again felt my eyes stinging with tears and my jaw quivering. I knew this time I was beyond a quick recovery so I ducked out the back hallway door and found my car where I sat for several minutes and wept.

15
MIRIAM

It had been over a decade since we'd identified dementia in Mom's life. She was in such a routine of steady, day-to-day life that I began to wonder if she would outlive me. She was currently in a "happy" mood phase and no longer depressed or cantankerous. In fact, she was 180 degrees opposite— peaceful, quiet and cheery, and the Millwood staff kept her upbeat with positive feedback. Experiencing this after her previous phase took a little getting used to.

One day I arrived and found Mom in the fireplace lounge all decked out to the hilt. Gone was the aqua-blue dress and holey white sweater and in its place was the nicest outfit I'd ever seen her wear. Not only that, but she wore a touch of lipstick and some nice jewelry. I guess I gawked a little too obviously, because when I turned back to the front desk, Jill was smirking.

"How did *that* happen?!" I asked.

"Isn't she cute? Maria is her new attendant in the dining hall and Laura just took a liking to her. A couple of days ago Maria asked if she could help her try on some new things, and she agreed!"

I was stunned. After three years of trying to make that happen, it had changed in one day, and, in the months to come, it never reverted.

It was just another one of those amazing reversals that I couldn't comprehend. When Dad died, she was 50; now she was 91 and had dodged *so* many bullets. And as I reflected on it one day, I again realized that when we sought answers to important decisions in her life, the answers were all almost always triggered by some catastrophic event.

It happened one evening about eight. I was settling into a good book when the phone rang.

"Hello, Mark? This is Margie at Millwood Assisted Living. I'm the night nurse. I just wanted to inform you that Laura fell a few minutes ago and we have an ambulance on the way."

"Oh, my goodness… thanks for letting me know... how'd it happen?"

"She was dancing a jig in the hallway, singing and acting silly when she tripped and fell. We don't know how, or if she is hurt, but by law we have to have her checked out."

"Thank you. That's fine. We'll head to emergency and meet them there."

Jamie and I threw a few things together before heading out. We arrived at the hospital just as the ambulance pulled in. After a lot of X-rays, tests and paperwork, about midnight we took her back to Millwood with a diagnosis of a cracked pelvis. We got her settled into bed and left, because the injury was serious but not debilitating. It was actually a godsend because it provided the opportunity for Millwood to officially declare that her needs had outgrown their ability to care for her. She was transferred to a nursing care facility for a brief rehab period with the option of electing to keep her there long term. We did.

As I faced move number five I realized that this would likely be the final act in Mom's dramatic life. She was now down to a few earthly possessions consisting of a narrow bed, a dresser and a wardrobe with a few pieces of clothing. We hung a cork board on the wall near her bed and filled it with a variety of photos of family and friends. Jamie added a vase of silk flowers for her dresser.

In spite of Mom's meager surroundings, Miriam Estates Nursing Home was a blessing. As a Catholic-owned facility, the staff and administration were totally committed to loving care and service to their patients. I was humbled by observing even the youngest staff members working long hours and facing daily challenges, including the difficult task of cleanup after incontinence issues.

One day I told the head nurse, "I can't believe how upbeat and kind these young people are as they care for the patients. I keep wondering why they aren't working at some high-paying, glamorous job!"

"Yes, we are very glad for them," she smiled.

"Where do you find them?" I continued.

Her reply was insightful. "Some just grow up knowing they want to help others. You're seeing the best of the best. The ones who can't take it don't stay."

Having Mom live at Miriam Estates brought a couple of

significant changes to our life. The one that really impacted my world was keeping up with visits. Driving to Miriam was a 50-mile round trip as opposed to what was 10 to Millwood. I could not visit as often and my Tuesday routine didn't work without fast food places nearby. (I considered eating at the nursing care center and quickly ditched that idea.) I was also reminded of how upside down the role between parent and child had become.

When our kids were small, we always inquired if they had to go potty before heading out somewhere. Now I had to do the same with Mom. I had to accept the fact that in many situations I was now the parent, she the child.

Since the tearful "last goodbye" Lisa experienced a decade earlier, she had seen Mom twice. The time for her visit to the States rolled around a third time, and even though Mom was in the nursing care home, in some respects she was doing better than the last time Lisa had visited. Since she didn't get much face time with Mom, Lisa was always ready to do special things with and for her—new clothes, gifts and lots of time to talk together.

I warned Lisa that Mom had reverted to a less-cheerful phase and conversation would be limited, but Lisa still dove right into information overload. On this visit she decided that Mom needed to have her hair done. It was primarily clean but un-styled, hanging to her shoulders. Lisa was all ready to reinvent things and change it to an impressive new style.

On the appointment day, we wheeled Mom to the in-house, all-glamour Miriam Hair Salon. I say "wheeled" because ever since her broken pelvis, she was given a contraption called a Merry Walker. It was constructed out of PVC pipe, probably invented by a person experienced in both healthcare and plumbing. It was a hybrid combination of wheelchair and walker. She could sit in it when she was tired, but if she wanted to motate, she could stand, surrounded by the pipe frame, and use it like a walker.

One thing I knew, dating back to my experience with Alexis at Millwood, was that messing with Mom's hair was inviting trouble. As Lisa and Jamie distracted Mom, I sidled up to Ms. Katherine-the-hairdresser and gave her the scoop on what she was about to experience. She replied, "Oh, I work with a lot of older people every day. It'll be fine. Don't worry."

Ok. Don't say I didn't warn you!

Contrary to the theory that dementia patients can experience complete memory loss, I know there are some things that are *never* forgotten.

Since I was the experienced one, I guided Mom into the chair and fielded her protests about not wanting her hair done. Lisa was still oblivious to the coming storm and was otherwise occupied with Jamie, chatting about the possibilities for the new do.

I decided to grit my teeth and wade into it.

"Mom, this is Katherine, and she's going to fix your hair." I tried to nonchalantly slide the term "fix" into her psyche, hoping it wouldn't cause any reaction. To the casual observer it may seem like a perfectly innocent word, but it was very carefully chosen. It was one that was designed to cancel out other problematic terms like *cut:* "Over my dead body!;" "*perm:* "I don't *want* it curly;" or *style:* "What's wrong with the way it is?"

"How come?" she asked as I sensed her stiffened body language.

"Well, it's time for it and it will look great!" I ventured.

"Well I don't want anybody messin' with my *hair!*"

Just then, Lisa, not satisfied with my meek and time-consuming approach, took things into her own hands and cut to the chase.

She swooped in from behind (ambushed would be more accurate) and said, "Momma, it's too long, and we're going to cut it pretty!"

OH NO! She used the C-word!

If you've ever been to a rodeo and seen a bull launch out of the chute gate, jumping and twisting and turning in an effort to shake off the rider, that scene would overlay very nicely into the next moment at the Miriam Estates Professional Hair Salon.

Mom's arms began flying under the cape in an effort to untie it. I sensed that by now Katherine had stepped aside and realized that although she was experienced, she was not *that* experienced. Fortunately, I had been standing next to the chair and was able to do a deft little blocking move to keep Mom from ejecting from her seat.

Now I was forced to select the Deceit Tool from my repertoire of behavioral artillery.

"It's okay, Mom. We won't cut it off! We just need to *wash* and *set* it." *Wash* and *set* were two notches below the alarm bell activated by the word *cut*.

"WELL, I DON'T WANT ANYONE MESSIN' WITH

168

MY HAIR!" she yelled.

Next, I selected the trusty Distraction Tool.

"Hey, Mom, do you want to get some lunch?" This 180 degree turn completely distracted her and helped dissipate her anxiety as smoothly as a binky in a baby's mouth. She wasn't completely fooled, but she couldn't assemble a reasonable response. Quickly, I kept the momentum going my way to maintain the upper hand.

"We can go to lunch in just a few minutes. Katherine is just about done!"

At this point Katherine looked scared spitless and needed some assurance. I winked at her and she eased in behind Mom. Lisa just slinked quietly back to the corner.

But, even best-laid plans fail. The instant ol' "I-work-with-a-lot-of-older-people" Katherine touched the hair, Mom's hand flew up and swiped the back of her head, knocking the comb from Katherine's fingers. To her credit, Katherine plowed ahead and got her hand slapped twice more before I called a truce.

Looking at Lisa, I said, "What do you want to do?"

Katherine took the question and said, "One thing we do in these cases is let it grow and pull it back into a pony tail."

Exhausted, but relieved to be done without bodily injury, we all retired to the dining room for a welcome lunch consisting of a pineapple and cottage cheese salad. I was especially grateful that Mom seemed to relish the yummy maraschino cherry that topped it all.

16
A NEW SONG

Some weeks later I was visiting Mom and found a small notebook that had somehow made it through all the moves. It was stuffed in the bottom of her wardrobe, under some slippers, along with a box of miscellaneous items. I opened the book with curiosity. Mom had kept a daily journal for over 40 years, so I was used to lots of rubber-banded little books that overflowed with receipts and extra paper scraps.

They detailed her every thought and activity. This one had the usual photos and clippings inserted throughout its pages. As I flipped through, my eyes scanned one entry and forwarded it to my consciousness. I suddenly stopped and backtracked to the page where I saw the words of a poem that seemed vaguely familiar…

There Was You
I wandered down a winding path
With no time or place in mind
I didn't know what life would bring
What kind of things I'd find.

Then there was you
So beautiful
    There was you
    So lovely
    There was you…
    There was you…
    Always you.

We wandered down a winding path
Together you and I,
Not knowing what the future held
For a love that reached so high.
(Chorus)

We wandered down a winding path
But then our paths diverged
We soon went our separate ways
Where love could not emerge.
(Chorus)

I wandered down a lonely path
With thoughts of days gone by
The years have passed and now they're gone
But love will never die.

"Oh my gosh! That's the song I've heard Mom sing all the time!" I said out loud. I had always wondered about its significance and now I could see it all clearly. But it still didn't hit me that they were original song lyrics until I saw the notation at the bottom:

172

Written by Laura Jensen Sanders, July 12, 1931. Christian James (C.J.) McKinney wrote the music. He and I sang it together all the time. We always thought we should publish it, but we never did. Darn! I guess it's just as well because we always thought of it as "our" song. I miss him!

It all fit together now! C.J. was Mom's first love. Once she married Tom, they'd drifted apart. I remembered the day she first moved to the mobile park. She said she and a friend used to sing this song as teenagers, and I now connected that to the Christmas cards I'd seen from Chris McKinney—not a woman but a *man!*

I sat back in silence. It took me awhile to process all of the ramifications. I suddenly realized that he had tried to reach out to her a couple of years ago! I wondered if I could ever locate Chris, or more importantly, if I should. Without knowing where he might be living, it was a difficult mystery to solve.

As the weeks went by, I focused on Mom's needs and once again forgot about Chris. I noticed that Mom was having visual recognition problems. The little indicators she used for recognizing me were failing because of my infrequent visits. She saw so many male attendants on different shifts that I soon became just another one of them.

As time went on, it wasn't just the visual part that continued to fail. By now her memory length was about one minute. Once I arrived and established who I was, she was okay for a while, but if I tested her by saying, "Did you know I'm Mark?—your son?" She'd laugh and say, "Really?"

173

"Yes, it's the same ol' me!" I'd tease.

When I asked "How are you doing today?" she'd smile and say, "Oh fine!"

On the next visit three weeks later it was much the same, but it gradually worsened. Once, I tested her by singing *There Was You*, but she responded only with a slight smile.

After a year at Miriam Estates, Mom's health stayed fairly constant. There was a definite nursing home atmosphere, especially in the dining hall. Mom wore a bib for the first time, and the food prescribed to her was labeled "soft food."

The label might as well have read "yuck food" because it was all I could do to even look at it. Mom just kind of played with it and ate only what she wanted—fruit paste or Jell-o which was hardly anything at all. But they let her snack on bottles of liquid nourishment all she wanted, so she seemed fine. She did lose weight gradually, eventually arriving at 89 pounds, down from 130 pounds in her younger years.

I was in the hallway once, talking to the shift nurse and caught Mom looking at an old gent who was tweedling past her in his wheelchair.

"Hey good lookin', whatcha got cookin'?"

I almost laughed out loud when I saw the dour look he returned her. Apparently, he wasn't ready for flirting at age 89. The nurse laughed too and said, "Laura's so fun!"

Mom had taken that greeting from an old song written by Hank Williams. She had a couple of other favorite songs she liked to throw around too. "Buy me some peanuts and Cracker Jacks!" was it for a while. Another was, "You are My Sunshine…" When I told Lisa about it, she said that the sunshine song was a favorite of Dad's that he had often sung to Mom. I understood then why it had stayed with her over the years.

I realized one day that her use of these fun song lyrics was becoming more frequent. She got the nickname of "Singing Sanders." My visits were spaced far enough apart that I was able to see marked decline in her each time I came. Trying to carry on a two-way conversation became nearly impossible.

It dawned on me one day that Mom was using song lyrics as a default for verbal communication. When memory loss eliminated her words and grasp of concepts, she would respond to a question with song lyrics that had remained in some corner of her brain.

More often than not, I would find her in bed, usually around noon. After driving the miles to be there, it was hard not to be able to see her awake, so sometimes I would gently wake her to have a little time together. That stage digressed to the point of always finding her in a darkened room, in bed, with her head under the covers and unresponsive. I wondered how much longer she could hold on.

My question was answered not long after that when I attended my monthly meeting with the healthcare administrators. This involved a group of about six of us, including a dietitian, nurses, a social services representative and the head administrator.

At first I didn't understand the seriousness of their conversation about congestion. I thought that meant Mom had heartburn. As they explained things further, I learned it was fluid retention around the heart, common among patients who lie in bed a lot.

I returned the following week, ahead of my usual schedule, to find Mom again in bed and unresponsive. The nurse asked to speak to me.

"Laura is not improving. There is a likelihood of congestive heart failure. There's not much we can do except keep her comfortable. I don't think it will be long now..."

Epilogue

After nearly 15 years of this adventure with dementia, it all ended rather quickly. I knew that congestive heart failure was a serious possibility and the hospice nurse at Miriam regularly kept me posted. I visited more frequently now, quietly watching Mom sleep in her little bed in the corner.

It was early December and as I watched her lie there peacefully, I thought of the times she must have watched me sleeping in my crib on our Colorado ranch. That day there were times when I could not tell if she was breathing. She was *so* thin and the beautiful complexion of her younger years was now sallow and drawn. I knew things couldn't go on much longer.

In mid-December my office gang decided to combine work with a little holiday fun and have our monthly meeting at a country Victorian house-turned-restaurant. It just happened to be a couple of miles from Miriam Estates. After an hour of lunch and chatter in an exquisite sitting room of the mansion, I suddenly heard my cell phone ring. I stepped out into the hallway to take the call.

"Hello, Mr. Sanders? This is Kerry. The charge nurse at Miriam?"

"Oh, sure! How are you?"

"I just wanted to let you know that Laura passed away a few minutes ago. I thought I'd tell you in case you want to come out to see her. There are some required things we must attend to. Then you can go in and see her if you want."

I had little in the way of a response. I just listened and tried to absorb the moment I'd known would come. Now that it had, I still felt it wasn't really happening. I felt like a huge section of my life and identity had just vanished.

I thanked Kerry and said I'd be right there. I returned to the party atmosphere. As I entered the room my colleagues sensed that something was wrong. After explaining what had happened they were compassionate and offered their help, but I felt I needed to go alone and quickly left to find my car.

I called Jamie first then drove through the beautiful countryside toward Miriam. Something about the cold but sunny day was calming, and I relished the peaceful moments to close this chapter of my life.

As I entered Mom's room, I did so with some reticence. I'm not a fan of open caskets or kissing the deceased, and I didn't know how I would feel about seeing her. But I knew I needed closure, so I just approached her tiny space as always. Her countenance was no different than on any of the previous days. In fact, if I hadn't known better, I might have assumed she was sleeping. But she was gone. She was simply absent from her body and in the presence of God whom she loved.

In the days following, Lisa and Dave flew to Orchard Heights. It was a beautiful but intimate service. After a day or two of catching up, we found ourselves in the mode we'd been in before—opening the door of a rented storage space in one last effort to liquidate some possessions.

Because Lisa had lived in distant lands for most of her adult life, she felt much more of an attachment to Mom's furniture than Dave or me. Since Lisa couldn't move it home, we elected to store it until she could decide what to do with it.

This day it was therapeutic for us to spend a little time together to share our memories of each treasured piece. There was a rocking chair, Mom and Dad's first bed frame and dresser, a dining room sideboard, a handmade magazine rack and shelves Dad had built and a variety of smaller items.

Just as before, I was drawn to the boxes containing personal effects. Mom had always meticulously recorded things and, of course, saved them. As we saw things of interest, we read them aloud and laughed or cried with the memories they brought.

One particular bundle of envelopes caught my eye. It had the obligatory rubber bands binding it together. For me, that was the time-tested alert that it held something interesting.

My pulse quickened as I comprehended the writing on several unopened envelopes. They bore the return addresses of Chris McKinney and others from Moondance Productions. I quickly sorted them by date and we opened them carefully. The first one was a short note from C.J.

April 10, 1945
Dear Laura,
I'm still in Nashville, and things are going well. The music business is fun but there are times when I wish I was home. Mostly I regret leaving

you and I wanted to write and apologize for the way I treated you. I guess I was just a fool and didn't know what I had. But I know you married Tom and I'm happy for you. I wish you the best.
C.J.

The next note was dated much later, August 1965, a couple of months after Dad's death and written on the inside of a sympathy card.

Dear Laura,
So sorry to hear the news of Tom's accident. I can't imagine how awful that must be for you. If there is anything I can do, just let me know. My address is 937 Cloverdale Ave., Walnut Creek, California.
C.J.

And again, in 1998:

Dear Laura,
I hope you are well. I have some news for you that I'm pretty excited about. I've stayed in touch with some of my contacts in Nashville and decided to see if they were interested in publishing our old song, "There Was You." Bob Bowman of Moondance Productions agreed to take it on. It's now out there now and doing okay. I'd like to see you if it's all right. I'm planning on heading north next month and would love to talk. I'll go over some of the legal stuff that I took care of so you can keep the rights to the lyrics you wrote.
Let me know if that works,
Always,
Chris (C.J.)

It all made sense now. Apparently C.J. had switched to his given name and Mom didn't recognize it after her memory started fading. As we looked at more of the notes, it was obvious that Chris had tried on several occasions to connect, but finally conceded that Mom did not remember him.

We began opening the Moondance Productions envelopes. They contained royalty checks, one after the other, enclosed in the neatly stacked, unopened envelopes. The checks were for one thousand dollars, fifteen hundred dollars and some over thirty-five hundred dollars.

All together they totaled $55,947.31. As we registered her death with the state, we transferred all of her Moondance mail to my address. Even though we'd already done that with her other business interests, we hadn't known about this one. Since Mom kept them in a box, they hadn't been returned as "address unknown," so no one caught it.

After closing all her affairs and settling the legalities involved, we were thankful for having at last discovered "the rest of the story."

In January I sent a thank you card to the Millwood staff and I drove out to Miriam to deliver a card to their staff and thank them personally. Along with the card I handed them a few boxes of peanuts and Cracker Jacks. We all had a good laugh.

Made in the USA
San Bernardino, CA
17 December 2014